DEVIL'S KISS

NICKOLE BRYAN

CONTENT WARNING (OR SHOPPING LIST, HOWEVER YOU CHOOSE TO INTERPRET IT)

The Devil's Kiss contains many graphic and religious elements that may be triggering for some readers. This is included but not limited to:

- *Drug use*
- *SA*
- *Mention of CSA (off page)*
- *Violence*
- *Death*
- *Mention of Suicide*
- *Rough Sex*
- *Language*
- *Blood Play*
- *Nudity*
- *Rape (off page)*
- *Various other graphic depictions of themes and material*

ENJOY AT YOUR OWN RISK (or pleasure)!

CHAPTER

ONE

SAMUEL

In the beginning, God created the Heavens and the Earth. That much of the Bible is true. However, like most everything else in the world, the rest is complete and total fucking bullshit. Centuries of old, uneducated men twisting the accounts of people who were there to witness the events that took place during that time has turned what should have been a short story (at best) into some elaborate, long-winded fairytale. And they didn't even do a good job of it. How they made the story of an omnipotent force playing around with the celestial equivalent of action figures into an entire fucking religion is beyond me. It is pretty genius, though, from a marketing standpoint. I wish I had a PR team like that.

The Bible did get one thing right, though. The Devil is real. And he is alive and well. But not in the Halloween-y, red skin and pitchfork way that many envision. No, I prefer a much more...aesthetically pleasing form than the description others have given me over the years. I was, after all, the most beautiful angel in all of creation. Still am, if you ask me. And I always will be, even if you don't ask.

Devil, Satan, Beelzebub, Lucifer. I've had many names throughout time. For the past several decades, however, I've gone by the name Samuel Delvine.

Over the years, I've taken on many roles. Not the ones most people give me credit for, mind you. Believe it or not, and despite what you may have heard, I am *not* the root of all evil. Neither is money, sex, or anything else like that for that matter. A person's God-given free will is the real evil of this world. Every choice a person makes, no matter how big or how small, is a fork in their proverbial road. For most people, their choices lead them through a good life with a peaceful rest when their days come to an end. For others, however, their choices bring them face-to-face with me. They sell their souls for trivial worldly pleasures and end up with nothing to look forward to in death but an endless void of darkness. Alone. Forever. Until eternity's end. Frankly, the thought of spending all of known and unknown time alone sounds like Heaven to me, but I digress.

The point I am making is this: No, I am not the monster that parents use to scare their children into behaving. Nor am I the great corrupter of morality, preying on the innocent and manipulating the weak. To put it quite simply, I am just a businessman. I provide a service, for a small fee, of course. The bartering of souls is nothing more than a career choice for me. And I am very good at my job.

In addition to the innumerable souls I have collected across the ages, I have also amassed a substantial amount of wealth. God may have cast me out of Heaven, condemning me to spend eternity walking the Earth amongst the very creatures I despised so much that I started a rebellion against the entire Heavenly Host, but never was it said that I had to serve out my sentence in poverty. The invention of the free-market system has been especially fruitful. I have found strip clubs to be a specialty of mine in recent years. I own more than three dozen in the US alone. My latest acquisition was purchased just a few weeks ago. Which is also why I am in this place, to begin with.

I flew out yesterday to assess the progress after one of my associates overseeing the remodeling of the building called me with more than a few concerns. I was going to stop by last night so I could be back on a plane headed home by this morning. However, I got distracted when I passed by a vacant lot on my way to the club.

The lot must have been abandoned for years. Probably decades. The crumbling ruins of a small building were all that remained among the weeds and overgrown patches of grass dotted between bare spots of earth. A few pieces of broken concrete outlined what used to be a sidewalk and foundation. Broken bottles and other trash were embedded in the ground from people trespassing over the years, driving the debris deeper into the dirt like some kind of urban archeological artifacts to be discovered hundreds of years from now. The neighborhood was overrun with hookers, pimps, and drug dealers. It was the perfect spot for a second club in this God-forsaken city. Just far enough away from the current location so as not to compete, but still in the part of town that would ensure that all of my potential clients here have access to the vices their desperate souls desire.

I stopped by the bank this morning and purchased the lot. Cash. Now, I am on my way there before heading to the club for the remainder of the evening. I want to do a quick assessment of the property before the sun goes down so I can determine how much work would need to be done before we can move forward with the construction of a second location. A quick walk-thru should be enough to tell what all needs to be taken care of. Then I can get the hell out of here, no pun intended.

As Drakin, my driver and right-hand man, pulls the car alongside the curb in front of the lot, I am more than slightly annoyed to see the once-empty lot is no longer vacant. "What the fuck?" I growl to myself. I don't wait for Drakin to come around to open my door. I am out of the car before he even has a chance to leave his seat.

Dozens of tents are scattered about the lot like a tiny campsite town. The residents of this city of squatters seem to all be gathering inside what little remains standing of the building in the middle of the lot. Confusion mixed with fear mars the faces of the ones who look up at me as I walk past them. I barely even notice them as I make my way to the building, the ground beneath my feet trembling with the force of my rage as my Italian leather loafers stomp across the dirty lot. I can feel the dead grass crunch beneath my feet as the smell of piss burns my flaring nostrils. I will have to remember to burn these shoes later. Probably the entire suit, just to get rid of the putrid smell.

Most everyone seems to be gathered around a singular figure; a hooded figure with their back to me as I approach. I may not be able to see their face, but I know a leader when

I see one. And this one is about to lead these vagrants off my fucking property.

I stop directly behind the stranger, who is kneeling down on one knee, talking to an old woman with matted hair and layer upon layer of dirty, ripped clothes. If I were capable of feeling physical pain, my palms would be stinging from my fingernails digging into them as I survey the sea of dirty faces staring at me right now. I clear my throat loudly, but the hooded figure doesn't even acknowledge my presence. At first, I was annoyed. Now, I am beyond fucking pissed at this blatant disrespect.

"Excuse me." Everyone in the immediate vicinity goes deathly quiet as I speak. "Exactly what the *fuck* do you think you are doing here?" My voice booms as I speak, shaking dust free from the deteriorating bricks of the building's remains.

The homeless woman recoils with an audible gasp despite there being at least six feet between us. The hooded figure, however, doesn't even flinch. Instead, the stranger, who has been silent up until now, releases an exasperated sigh as they straighten to their full height.

When I first noticed them as I was approaching, I could tell they were a bit on the scrawny side. Then again, most every person I encounter seems tiny next to me. At 6'7" and nearly 300 lbs. of mostly muscle, my human form is just as intimidating as my angelic one. This punk barely comes up to my chest. Probably some asshole teenager harassing the less fortunate for shits and giggles. Under normal circumstances, I'd be impressed at their bravado. Now, however, they are a nuisance that needs to be stomped out immediately.

I smile, baring my teeth as I cross my arms over my broad chest. The anticipation for the look on their face when they turn around and realize they are standing in the presence of the Devil himself. The stranger cracks their neck to each side. I have to fight the urge to double over in laughter. This little shit thinks he is about to go toe-to-toe with me. ME, of all people! Even if I were just some other mortal, there is no way this pathetic excuse of a human being could take me down in a fight.

The muscles of my biceps strain against the fabric of my shirt. Even though it was tailored to accommodate my size, the fine cotton was never meant to hold back the force of my wrath. I hear the threads as they start popping at the seams, the fabric holding on to itself desperately as a low growl rumbles in my chest.

The figure spins around on their heel to face me, the hood covering their head falling in the process. Or perhaps they pulled it down. I am too shocked by the face staring up at me to have noticed how the long, silky mane of silvery blonde hair tinted pink at the ends broke free of the confines of the hood that was just moments ago holding it back. Two gray-blue eyes bore into mine with all the intensity of a storm raging at sea. It's hard to tell under the dark, baggy clothes she is wearing, but judging by the way her fists slam against her narrow hips, it's hard to imagine this tiny creature weighs any more than my left leg.

Though she be but little, she is fierce.

Her mouth is set in a hard line, but it doesn't hide the fact she has lips that were made to suck a man's soul out of his body from his cock. My jaw twitches as an image of this girl on her knees in front of me doing just that, dances through my mind. Her mascara running down her face as I fuck that pretty little mouth of hers. The thought is unsettling, to say the very least.

And confusing.

I don't fuck humans. Never have. Never will. Their bodies are far too...delicate to withstand my desires. For this reason, I stick to my own kind to release my carnal urges with. Demons, goddesses, and other celestial beings satisfy me just fine whenever I feel the need to partake in my favorite of sins. Lamashtu is a particular favorite. The whole head of a lion thing being another myth cooked up by humans throughout the ages, of course. Her human form is one of the most beautiful I have seen in the entirety of creation.

Until now.

No angel, demon, god, or mortal creature holds a candle to the small siren glaring up at me right now.

"You're a woman," I snarl down at her through gritted teeth. No doubt, I look every bit the Hellhound that I am.

"No shit, Sherlock," she snaps back at me, rolling her eyes and giving absolutely zero fucks that I could break her in half at any second without any effort at all. I didn't think it was possible for my dick to get any harder than it already is, but here I stand corrected.

"What are you doing here, *woman*?" I repeat the word like it has personally offended me, making no attempt to hide my disgust. I am anything but disgusted with her, though.

Without breaking eye contact, she fishes around in the backpack that until now I hadn't even noticed she was holding. She pulls out a plastic baggie a moment later, slapping it against my chest with a smirk. "Sandwiches," she explains, a sarcastically sweet smile playing at the corners of her pink lips. My eyes leave hers only long enough to watch as the baggie falls to the ground at my feet when she lets it go. "Turkey with swiss is all I have left. If you want tuna salad, you're too late. Eddie got the last one." She points over her shoulder with her chin to a dirty old man sitting on the floor in the only remaining corner of the building. He flashes me a smile of rotten, yellow teeth as he holds up the last bite of the sandwich before popping it into his mouth. "And *don't* call me woman. I have a name."

Rage mixes with lust in my veins. No one has dared to speak to me like this. Ever. I simultaneously want to whip her until she bleeds and make her come until her voice is raw from screaming my name. The thought of doing each of those things to her makes my cock twitch equally in my pants. "Then what is it?" I retort, plucking the backpack from her hand and dropping it to the ground.

"I'm not telling you," she scoffs with a scowl as she crosses her arms over her chest. She looks me up and down, obviously unimpressed with what she sees. I bet if I were to strip naked right here in front of her, though, she wouldn't be so dismissive of my physical form. If there weren't so many other people around at this moment, I would be inclined to do just that. I'm sure the sight of my impressive cock would be enough to wipe that sour look off her face. If it wasn't, I can think of more than a few things that would.

My entire body is ready to explode. My skin burns with fury as my frustration, sexual and otherwise, rises to a boiling point. "If you are unwilling to tell me your name," I growl, leaning down over her as I try desperately to remain in control of the situation, "then you cannot complain about how I choose to address you."

"You could always just leave and not address me at all," she shrugs. Without another word, she turns on her heel, snatches her backpack off the ground, and resumes handing out the remaining bags of sandwiches to the others.

Did she just fucking dismiss me?!

"Why would I leave my own property when you and these vagrants are the ones trespassing?" I ask, following behind her like some kind of father trying to chase down their wayward child.

"Your property?" She repeats with a laugh, not even bothering to look at me as she hands a sandwich and a bottle of water to a dirty woman who looks to be in her mid-forties. The woman's eyes shift between the woman and mine as she slinks away and returns to her tent. "I think you've got the wrong address, Suit."

"I highly doubt that, considering I purchased it from the bank this morning." This gets her attention. She stops dead in her tracks as she turns around slowly to face me again. This time, however, traces of panic in her stormy eyes give her away. She's scared, but not of me. She's terrified of the power she now knows I hold over the fate of this desolate piece of property.

"This lot has been vacant for over a year," she says, trying to hide the tears forming in the corners of her eyes. She looks around at the people who are starting to gather around again after hearing this small piece of our conversation. She gives them a tight, reassuring smile, but I can tell she feels anything but assured.

"And by this time next month, it won't be," I explain,

finally feeling as if I have the upper hand with this woman. "So, you and your friends better pack up. You have until morning to find a new place to squat." This time, it's me with a satisfied smirk turning away from her, leaving her frozen in place with a shocked expression on her face.

"I'm not sure if you noticed from way up there, Sasquatch, but these people don't exactly have anywhere else to go," she explains as she races to catch up to me, my three or four steps equaling at least a dozen of her own.

"I really don't see how that concerns me. And judging by the way you said 'these people' and not 'us', I assume it really shouldn't concern you, either, if these people have somewhere else to go or not." I stop quickly, turning back around to face her as a final thought comes to mind. She almost runs right into me but stops herself before our bodies collide. "You know, woman," I continue, ignoring the way she stumbles two steps backwards to keep from falling on her perfectly tight ass. "You should apply to dance at my new club. I'm sure I could find a much better use for that smart mouth of yours other than talking."

"Like I would ever work for an asshole like you." She spits the words in my face, standing on her tiptoes in an effort to look more intimidating than she actually is.

"Asshole?" I scoff, ignoring her hypocrisy. "I prefer the name Samuel. Though, there are some who call me Master." I look her body up and down appreciatively, giving her a wink I know will piss her off even more than she already is.

"Master?" She doubles over with laughter as if I have just told her the funniest joke she has ever heard. "Like, you *own* people? Who the fuck calls themself Master?"

My teeth grind so hard that I am almost certain I might chip a tooth as she continues to laugh in my face. Well, as close to my face as she can get, considering our difference in height. Some of the others have started nervously chuckling as well, obviously noticing the effect this woman has had on me with her words alone. If they could only see the effect she has had on other parts of my body, they would no doubt be laughing much harder. I have never had someone control a situation like this in my entire existence. God, themself has never had this kind of power over me. And this mortal has done in the span of ten minutes what the Great Creator has never done in billions of years. Unacceptable.

Her laughter dies instantly in her throat as I grab the front of her black hoodie and pull her nose to nose with me. "I have owned more souls than you could count in ten pathetic lifetimes," I growl so only she can hear me, her eyes the size of dinner plates, as I pin her in place with my gaze. "And if you don't have these unwashed miscreants off my property by tomorrow, I'll own yours, too." I release my grasp on her clothing, but she doesn't run away as I expected her to.

"If you want these people to move," she growls back at me, the storm raging in her eyes as she pokes my chest for her delicate finger, "then you find somewhere for them to go."

With that, she turns on her heel and stomps off back to the remains of the building as the others follow behind her. I watch for a moment as she grabs her backpack off the ground and resumes passing out the remaining sandwiches. She stops only once to console an elderly woman who points at me with a shaky, knotted finger. She glances over her shoulder at me with a look that would wither a weaker man. Luckily for her, I am neither weak, nor a man. Not a mortal one, anyway.

She gives the woman a hug, no doubt feeding her some comforting lie about how everything will be okay and that they won't be going anywhere. I am only vaguely aware of Drakin coming to stand behind me as I continue to watch the way she interacts with these lowlifes. How she can stand to be around them, let alone touch them, is beyond me. They are worthless and have nothing to offer her in return for the meager meal she has provided for them. Even I wouldn't bargain for their pathetic souls. This woman is obviously not homeless or strung out like they are. Why does she give two shits about what happens to them?

"Sir?" Drakin says from behind me, pulling me from my thoughts.

"Yes, Drakin?" I sigh in exasperation at the entire situation.

"Michael is waiting at the club to speak with you."

"Oh, goodie." The words drip with as much sarcasm as I can muster. But I make no attempt to move. I am too entranced with watching the way this woman's hips move in the loose black sweatpants she wears. Idly, I wonder what she would look like in a fitted silk dress. Then, I wonder what she would look like wearing nothing at all. I am certain she is hiding a killer body under all of those baggy clothes. But the question still remains.

Why?

"Sir," he says again, this time with a little more urgency.

I shake my head, taking one last look at this mortal siren, and push my arrant thoughts aside. With any luck, I'll never have to see her again, which is for the best. For both of our sakes.

"Yes, I suppose we should get going," I say, turning and walking back to the waiting car. "Wouldn't want to keep my dear brother waiting, now would we."

TWO

SAMUEL

The sun has barely set as Drakin pulls the car to the curb in front of the building. The lingering light clings to the bottom of the clouds like a man desperately clinging to life as the blackness of death washes over him. The corners of my lips curl up into an approving smile as I peer out the window up at the front of the building. I can already see a marked improvement from my first visit before I even set foot outside the car.

The once disgusting brick exterior has been cleaned and painted black. When night falls, the building will blend into the night like a shadow. The tacky flashing neon sign has been replaced with one much more discrete and sleeker. Even the sidewalk looks better now since I have had security placed outside the main entrance to keep the winos and drug dealers from littering it with both their trash and their existence. I chuckle to myself as Drakin opens my door, and I step out into the cool evening air.

Eden. How fitting.

The moment I saw the name of the club, I knew I had

to have it. This Eden will be the paradise that the garden God built never was. And no one will be cast out of this one, so long as they can pay the price to stay.

Walking inside, I am even more impressed with the progress that has been made in such a short amount of time. The lights and main stage have been replaced. Brand new tables and chairs surround the main stage. Freshly reupholstered booths form small half-circles around two smaller stages to each side of the main one. New carpet that no longer smells of vomit and stale alcohol lines the hallway leading back to the private VIP rooms. All of this is but further proof that with the proper motivation and an unlimited bank account, a person can accomplish almost anything nearly immediately.

As I stand near the stairs leading up to the main office and survey the club, I can't help but marvel at how this place has been completely transformed in just a few weeks' time. What was once little more than a hole-in-the-wall club, will soon be the premier adult entertainment establishment of its kind in the state. Even the clientele gathered around the main stage is of a higher quality than it previously was. Sure, a few blue-collar boys are still mingled in, but it makes my smile grow wider when I see all the suits and leather loafers mixed in with dirty jeans and steel-toed work boots.

The girls seem happier, too. The sight of $100 bills mixed with the singles and fives will do that. I had to clean house with the staff, as well, when I took over. I might be the Devil, but I run a tight ship with a zero tolerance for drugs or thieves. There is also no "extra work" allowed on my watch. The last thing I wanted was to have cops start sniffing around because the customers were getting more than a dance in the back rooms. Not that I couldn't afford to pay them off, but it was a headache I had no intention of dealing with.

As I scan the room one last time before heading upstairs to my office, I catch a glimpse of Eve as she maneuvers her way gracefully through the crowd. Her long, dark hair falls in loose waves over her chest, hiding her bare breasts from view. Not that I haven't seen them on more than a few occasions. The white thong and heels she wears compliment her deeply tanned skin perfectly. Her long lashes flutter as her hazel brown eyes convey wordlessly everything she doesn't have to say to these men as she passes them by. Eve looks nothing like the white-washed depictions I've seen in countless murals and paintings throughout the centuries. Something she personally finds hilarious.

Another thing that book got wrong was what happened to Eve after she ate that apple. Yes, she and Adam were forced to leave Paradise for disobeying God. He, however, groveled at God's feet and was rewarded for it. Eve, on the other hand, refused to beg forgiveness for her arbitrary transgression. So, instead of regaining favor in God's eyes, she was punished. Most of the punishments were also handed down to every other woman who has come since her. One curse, however, was hers alone to bear. Immortality. For her disobedience, Eve will never die, forever denied a peaceful rest after her long years.

I found her a few centuries after her expulsion from the Garden. She was wandering aimlessly through the world with no purpose or idea of what to do with her endless days. Since then, she has become one of my closest friends and business partners.

"Have Eve meet me in my office," I say to Drakin over the thumping bass of the music. "I want a full report on how the old girls are acclimating to the changes. And I want to know how the new girls are working out."

He gives me a curt nod before turning and walking to the end of the bar to wait for Eve to finish her rounds. I chuckle to myself as the tinkling of her laughter floats above the music to my ears. I shake my head before turning away from her, sitting in some guy's lap as he no doubt is stuffing half his life savings into her garter. Eve may look innocent, but she is the Mother of Seduction. These men will happily hand over entire paychecks for even the *chance* to spend a night with her. And when she rejected them, they would still worship at her feet, thanking her for that as well.

The music started to fade below me as I climbed the stairs to my office. I made sure to leave strict instructions with the contractors that the second floor was to be made completely soundproof. Seems they were successful in that task. But the near silence leads to another problem. Without the blare of the music to drown out my thoughts, a certain siren in sweatpants creeps back into my mind. The thought is just as annoying as her smartass mouth was. Her perfect, sexy, smartass mouth.

I crack my neck to both sides as I open the door to my office, hoping that these thoughts of that woman will soon fade. They were counterproductive, to say the very least. I was a busy man. Too busy to waste my time with lustful thoughts of a woman I would never see again. I never even got her name.

The upstairs office of Eden overlooked the entire main floor. A giant one-way mirrored window behind my desk allowed me to see everything. The private VIP rooms had all been outfitted with closed-circuit cameras, their feeds displayed on a large T.V. screen on the wall to the left of my desk. Eve was my eyes and ears in the dressing rooms, which meant there wasn't a single square inch of this building that I was unaware of. There wouldn't be a move made by anyone, patron or staff, that I couldn't see.

"Nothing but sin for as far as the eye can see." Michael's deep voice echoes off the glass, making it feel like he is surrounding me inside this room as I close the door of the office behind me. "For someone who hated them more than anyone else in existence, you sure have found a way to fit in amongst these mortals." He doesn't even turn to face me as he insults me. Instead, he continues to stare out the glass at the girl on stage as she contorts her body around the pole.

Michael has always been an asshole. A rather large asshole, even in his human form. His mortal body stands as tall as mine, and even with his back to me, I can see the muscles flexing under his fitted t-shirt. He's tense, that much I can tell.

"I wouldn't call what I do fitting in," I explain flatly as I shrug out of my suit jacket and carefully hang it on the hook on the back of the door. "More like making the best of an unjust prison sentence."

"You tried to overthrow God," he seethes as he turns to face me, his eyes burning with the barely contained rage he obviously still feels towards me for my actions more than a few millennia ago. "Your sentence should have been death, not exile."

"Do you really plan on holding this grudge forever, brother?" I ask, already bored with this conversation as I roll up the sleeves of my shirt in preparation of the fight I am sure is about to take place.

"I am the Flaming Sword of God, Samuel," he says with a calm that betrays the self-satisfied smirk as it spreads slowly across his face. "Holding a grudge is what I do."

I want nothing more than to wipe that look off his face right now. "If you're looking for a fight, Michael, do you mind if we take it outside?" My jaw clenches so tightly with anger that I am certain I am about to chip a tooth. "I would hate to destroy the building after I just sank hundreds of thousands of dollars into renovating it."

Michael chuckles smugly to himself. "No need for that," he snorts. "We both know how it would end, anyway. The same way it did last time."

"With me being pulled off of you right before I ripped your fucking wings off?!" We both growled as I stomped across the floor until I was nose to nose with my brother. I was beyond angry at this point. I was furious. No one, not a single one of my siblings, had even bothered to visit me in all the years I had been down here. The fact that he was here now, the one I was closest to when I was one of them, spouting off his mouth to me as if he was any less evil than I am, turned my vision red.

I feel my nostrils flare as I stare my brother down. Neither of us says a word for a long moment. The room is like a powder keg awaiting the smallest spark to set it off in a fiery explosion. But then he does something I did not expect. He blinks.

Michael releases a heavy sigh as he steps back and lowers his eyes. "I did not come here to fight with you."

"Then why did you come here?" I snap, still not trusting his sudden change in demeanor.

"I came to warn you." I roll my eyes and scoff as he raises his eyes back to meet mine. What could he possibly have to warn me about? I'm the goddamn Devil, for fuck's sake. What do I have to be afraid of? "You're going to die soon, brother," he continues, as if he heard my unspoken question. "I have seen a vision of your death."

This gets my attention.

"Yes, I gathered that when you said I was going to die soon." I do my best to keep the nervousness out of my voice. Truth be told, the fact that Michael had foreseen my doom was very concerning indeed. Michael had a gift of foresight. And his visions were never wrong. "What exactly did you see?"

"You," he says as his eyes gloss over in a white sheen, his vision taking over his eyes. "Lost in a clouded sea as the life drains from your earthly body."

I swallow hard as his eyes return to their normal emerald green color. He shakes his head to clear his mind of the vision that has obviously unnerved him enough to come see me. I haven't seen or spoken to Michael since he was ordered to cast me out of Heaven. For him to be here now, he must have seen more than he is telling me.

"So, I avoid the beach for a while," I say, trying to play it off as if I am not just as concerned as he is. "Problem solved."

"You know as well as I do that you can't escape this."

"There's nothing to escape," I explain as I walk over to

the bar set up just under the massive screen displaying the feeds from the private rooms. "In case you have forgotten, I cannot drown. So, your vision is wrong." I pour two glasses of the strongest whiskey I have from the decanter before turning and offering one to him with a smile on my face. "You were bound to get one wrong eventually."

"I'm never wrong."

"You are this time."

"Then why are you afraid?"

"Who said I am?"

"Your eyes are screaming your fear."

I don't argue his assumption. Because there would be no need. He's right. I am afraid. But I am also just cocky enough to know I can avoid the death he has seen by simply adjusting a few plans.

"Even if you're right, which I am certain you are not, why come to warn me?" This is a question that I cannot seem to answer myself.

"It's not your death that I am here to warn you about," he says, finally taking the glass but setting it aside on my desk without drinking it. "It's the cause."

"Yes," I say, rolling my eyes again before taking a long drink from my own glass. "Clouded ocean. Life draining. Blah blah blah."

"You think you cannot die." It's not a question, but rather a statement.

"I know I cannot die. I am still an angel, after all." His riddles and half-truths are really starting to get under my skin.

"Anything can die, Samuel. And you will freely give your life for another. That is what I have seen."

I throw my head back in barking laughter, all fear from hearing his vision evaporating with the sound. "There is not a soul on this earth, nor in Heaven that I would lay down my life for."

"There will be." He speaks with confidence. "And death will come for you sooner than even you realize."

I open my mouth to speak again, but a soft knock at the door interrupts me before I can. Eve opens the door and steps inside, not bothering to wait for an invitation. "You sent for me," she says as she closes the door behind her. She suddenly stops short when her eyes meet Michael's before she lowers them to the floor, folding her arms over her chest to cover her still-bare breasts from view.

Michael swallows hard as his eyes rake over her body. He opens his mouth to speak, but no words come out. He closes it a moment later without a sound.

No one says a word for what feels like an eternity. I clear my throat just to break the silence. "Eve, you remember my brother, Michael," I say, trying to relieve the sudden awkward tension that has filled the room.

"Yes," he says, the word a breath on his lips.

"I remember him throwing me out of the Garden on my ass," she snaps, raising her eyes to his again, the dark brown color replaced with fiery red hatred.

Michael doesn't react. At least not noticeably. I, however, can see the way he recoils ever so slightly at her words. It's as if she reached out and physically slapped him in the face.

Interesting.

"I should be going," he says, grabbing his leather coat from the back of the chair behind the desk and hurrying out of the room. Before he leaves, he brushes against Eve's shoulder, and I can swear I hear a faint moan escape her lips at the contact. Michael seems to notice it as well, freezing momentarily with his hand on the doorknob. His fingers flex, as if he is arguing with himself about if he should stay or if he should leave. A moment later, he leaves without another word. The part of him that said leave must have won that fight.

"What was all that about?" I ask Eve as soon as the door clicks closed behind Michael. A flash of light from under the door tells me that he didn't even wait until he was outside to return back home.

"It was nothing," she sighs, unable to make eye contact with me as she says the words and drops her arms back to her sides. Her entire body visibly relaxes, her slender shoulders dropping as the tension leaves them.

"Didn't seem like nothing from where I'm standing."

"Did you need something from me, Samuel?" she asks as she rakes her hand through her long hair. Obviously, there is more going on between her and Michael than she has ever told me, but she won't tell me anymore right now.

"We will definitely be revisiting this...interaction at a later time," I explain as I walk around my desk and take my seat. "How are the girls adjusting to the changes?"

"Everyone that you kept on board seems pleased so far," she explains, switching seamlessly into business mode as she walks over to the bar and pours herself a drink. Not the whiskey I had poured for myself and Michael, though. Eve was never much of a hard drinker. She opts for a glass of the chilled champagne instead, before taking a seat on the leather couch against the opposite wall. "The girls are making three times as much money as they were before, even on the slow nights."

"Perfect." I steeple my fingers under my chin as my computer screen comes to life in front of me. "What about the clientele?" I ask as I go over the numbers from the past two weeks.

"That was a bit more drastic of a change," she explains before taking a long sip from her glass. "A fair number of the previous customer base did not like the new rules barring prostitution. It got a little rough with a few of them at first."

"How rough?"

"Nothing I couldn't handle." The wicked smile she gives me is all the answer I need. Eve could be almost as sadistic as me at times. If there were any issues with some of the customers, I am confident she took care of them in a way only she could.

Turning in my chair to look out the window at the main stage, I see the girl Michael was watching as she gathers the last of the money that has been thrown on stage during her set and makes her exit while the DJ announces the next dancer. The girl is beautiful. Dark, raven hair and skin the color of porcelain. Idly, I think how perfect it would look with a few marks from my whip across her back. I might not fuck human women, but I did appreciate their beauty at times. And after the day that I have had, a private dance before summoning someone more suitable for my needs might be just what the devil ordered.

"Is my private room finished yet?" I had the contractors add a private room just for me across the hall from my office. I hadn't had the chance to inspect it yet, but there was no time like the present.

"I did the final walk-through of it just this morning."

"Perfect," I smile, still watching the girl as she disappears behind the curtain offstage.

The lights dim as the shadowy outline of the next dancer walks on stage. I am about to turn away and instruct Eve to send the raven-haired girl up to my private room when the lights come back on, and I see the new dancer on stage.

No fucking way.

I knew she was hiding a killer body under those sweats, I just never thought I would see that body dancing around a pole on the main stage of my club. This woman is full of surprises, it would seem.

"Who is that woman?" I ask, rising to my feet to get a better look as she dances. Her hips move in time with the music I cannot hear as more men come to gather around the stage. Some of them, I notice, abandon the lap dances from the girls working the floor just to watch her.

I can see why.

Her skin glitters in the light, most likely from some kind of body gel she applied backstage. The white bra and thong set, along with the gold headband she wears, makes her look like some kind of angel. Well, the cartoonish version of what mortals think angels look like, anyway. A saint amongst the sinners. And this crowd is eating it up.

I sense Eve as she comes to stand beside me, but I don't look away from this angel on the stage. "Her?" she asks incredulously. "Angelique I believe is the name she goes by."

"I don't want her stage name," I correct, feeling

something rise in my chest that I have never felt before. All these men are watching her as she dances. They are watching something they have no business seeing. Not a single one of them is worthy of looking at her this way.

"Seraphine," Eve says. "Her name is Seraphine."

Of course she would have an angelic name.

Her hips move as she gives one of the men a wink while simultaneously unclasping her bra. A low growl rumbles in my chest. She should not be on that stage. They should not be seeing what is *mine.*

I turn away from the window before she drops the dainty garment from her fingers into the crowd of drooling heathens. I stomp across the floor, yanking the door open before slamming it closed behind me. I don't wait for Eve to answer my command. This feeling inside is foreign. And it pisses me off.

Never in my eternal life have I ever laid claim to a mortal the way I am about to claim this woman.

"Bring her to me."

THREE

I did my best not to show how pissed off I was while I finished handing out the food and water I had brought to the lot this afternoon, but my jaw was really starting to ache from clenching it so tightly for the last half hour. I groaned to myself as I tried to force myself to relax, at least a little before I made it to work. No way I was going to make the amount of tips I needed to make tonight if I walked in with an expression that suggested I was ready to rip the balls off of everyone in sight. I pulled my phone out of my back pocket to check the time as I turned the corner down the alley that led to the back entrance to the club.

Shit.

I was forty-five minutes late. Again. I could have taken the bus or a cab, but I had spent the last of my cash on the stuff to make the sandwiches. I would be broke until next week if I didn't make some serious tips tonight. I sighed heavily while I ran through the mental list of items in my pantry, dividing them up in my mind so that I could stretch them out as long as possible to avoid going grocery shopping.

To make things even better, the new owner was supposed to be in tonight to check up on his investment. I probably wouldn't even see the guy, but this was the third night in a row that I was late. Even though my immediate boss was great and understood why I was having trouble getting in on time, I knew she wouldn't put up with my constant tardiness forever. I needed a car, and I needed one badly. But it was hard to save when I was struggling to make enough to pay rent every month, let alone food and utilities.

As if on cue, my stomach growled and gurgled with hunger as I opened the back door to Eden, the club I had just started dancing at a couple of weeks ago. I had planned on saving one of the sandwiches I had made for myself to have during my break, but there were more people than I anticipated at the lot. Guess word got out quickly when I told Maggie I had found a place for everyone to make camp at for a while until the shelter was able to open back up. *If* it ever opened back up.

Stupid politicians that sit behind stupid desks and make stupid decisions that cut stupid budgets for places like the shelter and ruin the lives of people who are just trying to survive. And stupid fucking rich assholes who wear stupid suits, although well-taylored and perfectly fitted to accentuate every hard muscle on their body, that probably cost more money than it would take to keep the shelter up and running for at least a year. That lot was the perfect spot for everyone to camp at until I could figure out a more permanent solution. That is, until that gazillionaire son of a bitch showed up saying he had purchased it and ruined everything. Now, I was going to have to find somewhere else for everyone who used to live at the shelter to stay. And I had less than 24 hours to do so.

Peeking around the corner of the changing area, I hoped no one had noticed yet that I was once again late. I would have texted or called Eve to let her know, but my phone was out of minutes. I wasn't going to have the funds to refill it, though, for at least a few more days.

I walked in and set my bag down next to my locker when I saw the coast was clear, releasing a sigh of relief and trying to ignore the hunger pains in my belly. Maybe I could at least get some fruit from the bar to hold me over until I could get back home and make some microwave soup or something. As I started stripping out of the sweats I had on and changing into the white string bikini I had packed for tonight, I heard the heavy security door that led out onto the main floor open before slamming shut again. Looking up, I saw the one friend I had managed to make in the few weeks I had been dancing here, Charmaine, walk into the room as she counted the stack of singles in her hand.

"How's it looking out there, Char?" I asked as I finished tying my top and adjusting it into place.

"Kind of a slow start, but looks like it's picking up now that the market has closed and the factories have let out." Charmaine was as close to the girl-next-door type I had ever seen before. She had long, silky blonde hair that looked like spun gold when the light hit it just right. Her big, blue doe-eyes reminded me of Old Hollywood actresses. She was tall, but not too tall; thin but not too thin. She had curves in all the right places. Even her voice sounded as innocent as a church mouse. Anyone who saw her walking down the street would never guess in a million years that she took her clothes off for money. The fact that she was just as sweet and personable as she looked made things even better. The guys who came in here lined up when she danced just to get a peek at what she hid under that innocent facade. And every one of them wanted to corrupt that innocence.

"Any sign of the new boss yet?"

"Not that I've seen," she answered as she flopped down on the couch behind me. "But I just spent the last hour working the side stage and giving some investment banker a private dance. Wasn't exactly watching the front door, if you know what I mean." I see the wink and little smirk she gives me as I watch her in the mirror hanging inside my locker.

"I thought the new boss said no *extra services*," I laugh, not caring one bit that my friend made a little cash on the side with her body. If anyone was in no position to judge, it was most definitely me.

"I followed the new rules to the letter," she smiled wickedly, reminding me that she was nowhere near as innocent as her looks suggested. "I never laid a finger on the guy, and he never touched me. He did, however, touch himself while I gave some...let's call it gentle encouragement."

"Malicious compliance," I smiled back at her in the mirror as I grabbed the gold chain I had made into a sort of halo out of some old thrift store jewelry. "I love it."

Both of us double over in laughter as I hear the door open and shut again. "What's so fucking funny in here?" I closed my eyes and stifled the groan in my throat at the sound of Jenna's voice. If Charmaine was the best friend I have made since starting here, then Jenna was definitely the worst enemy. "Seraphine," she said with a saccharine-sweet smile as I narrowed my eyes at her condescending tone, "'bout time you showed up. Thought I was going to have to cover your spot. Again."

"I had a little delay when I was on my way in," I snapped back at her, even though it was really none of her business to begin with.

"What could have possibly held you up for almost an hour? Car trouble?" She laughed at her snide little joke. It was no secret that I had a transportation issue at the moment, and Jenna loved to remind me about my situation every chance she could.

"Something like that."

I wasn't about to tell her or anyone about what I did in my free time. If they knew I spent over half of my income helping the people from the shelter, they would ask why. That was a conversation I was not ready to have just yet. No matter what, it always ended the same way whenever anyone found out about who I used to be and what I used to do. First came pity, then came trying to sympathize, and lastly, they either disappeared from my life entirely or stuck around just to rub my past in my face. Even Charmaine wouldn't be able to understand, so I kept the details of my life outside these walls to a minimum.

"You should really try changing up your wardrobe, Seraphine," Jenna said as she leaned over one of the makeup tables and reapplied her lip gloss. "The guys would probably tip you more if they saw you in something other than that tired old angel get up every night."

I gritted my teeth, fighting the urge to fall for the bait she was luring me in with. As I watched her from the corner of my eye as I finished getting my wings into place, I couldn't help but think how much Jenna looked like the stereotypical stripper. She had an orange-looking fake tan that was at least three shades too dark for her. Her tits were too big for her tall and definitely substance-sustained thin frame. They barely moved when she danced, as well. Evidence of a not-so-subtle boob job. Even her overprocessed, dark brown hair looked cheap and fake. She might have had a killer body with an ass you could bounce a quarter off of, but the sum of all her parts made her one of the ugliest people I had ever had the misfortune to meet.

I closed my eyes and took a deep, calming breath as I heard the DJ calling Jenna's name in one of his long-winded introductions. She sashayed away, blowing Charmaine a kiss as Char flipped her the bird. I choked on the laughter that threatened to bubble up inside of me as I watched Jenna scowl and then stomp off to get on stage.

I just needed to finish getting ready then, hopefully, I wouldn't have to deal with Jenna anymore for the rest of the night. Nothing good would come from me snapping back at her backhanded advice right now, anyway. Even if I did agree with her, it wouldn't really matter. This was the only thing I currently owned that would be suitable for stripping.

"Don't let that bitch get to you," Charmaine says, standing from her spot on the couch, as we hear Jenna's stage set start. She notices me struggling to get the harness fastened for my wings. These things have definitely seen better days. Hopefully, they can hold out a little bit longer for me, though. With everything else going on, I know I won't be able to replace them any time soon, if ever.

Charmaine starts helping me without me having to ask. That's just the kind of person she is. Unlike that jackass I met today.

My jaw tightens in anger at the mere thought of that asshole. That rich, sexy asshole. Something else starts tightening as I think about the way he towered over me in that suit, the way his muscles flexed under the fine fabric, the way he looked at me like he couldn't decide if he wanted to kill me or fuck me. My clit aches as my pussy clamps down on nothing; images of what a man like him would be like in bed play on a loop inside my head. I instantly hate myself as I rub my thighs together while my treacherous body responds to the thought of him in a way it most certainly should not be responding. I know it's been a while, but that should not be the first guy to get me wet like this. Even if he was hands down the hottest man I have ever laid eyes on, he was still a jerk. And that jerk now owned the property I had planned on using to help the people from the shelter.

He said I had until tomorrow to move them, but with the only shelter in ten miles closed indefinitely, there wasn't anywhere for everyone to go. Not unless I thought of a plan and thought of it fast. Unfortunately, the only thing I seemed to want to think about right now was that guy. Maybe I could talk to him tomorrow and work something out. If that conversation went the same way as the one today, however, then I doubt he would be willing to discuss any kind of compromise.

There was another option to get him to be more flexible with the timeline he set to get everyone moved off the lot. I swore I would never do anything like that again, but this was different than all the times I had done it in the past. This wouldn't be for selfish reasons. I could do it, if it meant they would get to stay for a while longer.

I felt my chest starting to tighten up at the thought of what I was most likely going to have to do in order to save those people from being forced off the property. My ears started ringing with a high-pitched whining noise that drowned out everything else around me as tunnel vision started to set in. I felt my legs get weak, so weak I thought for a second I might fall over.

"Seraphine!" Charmine nearly screams my name, snapping me out of the panic attack.

I suck in a deep breath, nearly choking on the air. I didn't even realize I had stopped breathing until I felt the precious air being dragged back into my starved lungs. Stars danced in front of my eyes as my vision slowly returned to normal. It's been months since I had had a panic attack like this. Then again, it's been that long since I had done the things I was just considering. No way my plan to seduce him would work if I couldn't get this under control.

"You okay?" Charmaine's voice is laced with concern as she places a bottle of water in my hand.

"Yeah," I reassure her with as genuine a smile as I can muster as I take a sip from the bottle, desperately wishing it was something stronger than water. "Just got a bit dizzy for a second."

"Have you eaten today?" she asks, folding her arms over her chest and looking at me like a disapproving mother scolding a child.

"Yeah, of course," I lie, avoiding eye contact as I grab my makeup from my bag and start applying my glitter. I can hear the muted sound of Jenna's music as the final bars play. "It's nothing. Really," I explain, knowing she knows I am lying as I slip my heels on.

"I'll have Armando run get you a cheeseburger. It'll be waiting for you when you get done with your set," she calls after me as I make my way to the stage door. "I expect you to eat it, missy!"

I chuckle softly to myself as I open the door and make my way to the stage. She may be a few years younger than I am, but Charmaine has been more of a mother figure to me in the few weeks that I have known her than my actual mother was my entire life.

I adjust my homemade halo one last time just behind the black curtain separating the door to the dressing room from the stage as the DJ goes into his long intro to give Jenna time to collect the cash from the stage the men have thrown at her before she makes her exit. Her icy gaze raked me from head to toe and back again as she walked off stage past me. Her deep brown eyes were almost glacial with cold hatred. I ignore her as best I can, my mind already drifting to that place inside me it always goes to when I dance.

The warmth always starts in my belly as I step onto the stage, spreading across every inch of my skin like a wildfire.

"Call the missus and tell her you are at church! Come all ye faithful and worship at the feet of Angel!" Knowing no one else can see my face at this moment, I can't help but roll my eyes at Dean's, the DJ for the night, introduction of me.

The lights slowly start to come up as my music starts to float across the stage. *Unholy* by Sam Smith. Perfect song for my set. The music flows through my body as I move, undulating my hips with the rhythm. The smile that spreads across my face is anything but holy as I look out into the sea of faces watching me as I move. I work the pole as if it is an extension of my body. I always feel the most powerful when I am on stage. I am the one in control. No one else.

Most people look at stripping as exploitation of the dancer, forcing them to use their bodies to get paid. In reality, however, I'm not the one being exploited. Every move I make when I dance is a manipulation of the men throwing their hard-earned money at my feet. Every wink, every flirtatious smile, every move I make is carefully crafted to elicit the exact response I want from them. For the three and a half minutes I am on this stage, I am their goddess. And they worship me exactly how I tell them to.

If sex really does sell, then I am the goddamn CEO of this place. No one does it better than I do.

Reaching behind me, I start to untie my top, careful not to expose too much too soon. The longer I tease, the more they are willing to pay. As I finally let the top fall to the floor, I run the tips of my fingers across my sensitive nipples. They instantly harden into diamond-hard peaks as I expose my bare tits to the crowd of men gathered around the stage. It feels good to be the one in control as I finish my dance. I am not doing this for anyone else but me. Not these men. And definitely not for my next fix. This is all for me.

As my music starts to fade out and I finish my set, a final flurry of cash is thrown onto the stage. I scoop it up while Dean buys me some time by talking about some of the drink specials for the night. I walk off stage with my fistfuls of wadded-up bills and head back towards the dressing room to put it in my locker before heading out onto the floor to try to score some lap dances. I smile politely but don't speak to the next girl heading on stage, blanking completely on her name.

Walking into the dressing room, I stuff the cash into my bag in my locker and turn around to see a bag from the burger joint across the street with my name written in big, bold black letters across the brown paper. I smile and roll my eyes, shutting my locker door as I turn and snatch the bag up. I flop down on the couch and dig out the burger. I'm pretty sure I took a bite out of some of the wrapper as well when I took the first huge bite. My stomach growls in appreciation as I ferociously devour the entire thing as quickly as possible, stopping to shove a few fries in my mouth between bites of burger. I didn't realize how hungry I really was until I started eating. I pause for a second as a memory of the last time I had eaten a meal from this place comes to mind. It was out of the dumpster behind the building when I was high.

The sound of the door opening and clanking shut again pulls me from the depressing memory. "Hey, Eve," I say to my boss as she walks in.

Eve was naked except for a barely-there thong, as per usual for her. I swear, Eve was more comfortable being naked than she ever was fully clothed. Even the thong she was required to wear seemed to irritate her. Nude or not, however, she was always sweet and kind to me. I liked her a lot, and from what I had heard, she had been brought in by the new owner to clean the place up when he took over. Seems like she had done a really good job of that in just a short amount of time. No small feat, judging from the stories the few remaining dancers had mentioned of how poorly managed the club was before her arrival.

"Finished with your first set?" she asked, standing over me as I tossed the now empty burger wrapper back in the bag.

"Yep," I answered. "Just about to head onto the floor for a while."

"Actually," she started, twisting her fingers in front of her as she shifted her weight from one foot to the other.

Shit.

I suddenly felt the meal I had just eaten starting to rise in the back of my throat. I swallowed hard as a million scenarios played out in my head. I guess my tardiness had finally caught up to me. Eve's tolerance had obviously run out, and I was about to get fired from the first legit job I had ever had.

"The boss wants to talk to you."

"About what?" I asked, already knowing what was coming. Guess the new owner wants to be the one to do the honors himself.

"I-I don't really know," she replied, looking just as confused as I was.

"Oookaayyyyy."

"He's waiting for you upstairs in his private suite." She

turned to walk away, but stopped and turned back around to face me. "I would hurry if I were you. I've known Samuel for...well, let's just say I've known him a long time. He's not the kind of man you want to keep waiting."

"Am I in trouble or something?"

Eve opens her mouth, but closes it again before answering. Her brows furrow like she is trying to figure out a really hard riddle or something. She doesn't say another word, however, mumbling something under her breath in a language I don't understand as she just turns and walks out the door.

I wipe my mouth one last time with a napkin as I stand, tossing the napkin and bag in the trash as I walk out, still completely confused by the interaction I had just experienced with Eve. If I am in trouble, why would the owner want to see me instead of just letting his manager handle it herself? I had already been informed when I started working here that the owner was not exactly a hands-on kind of guy, and I probably would never even meet him. So why was he asking to speak to me personally in private?

It took me more than a few minutes to make it to the staircase that led to the upstairs area. It was on the opposite side of the club from the stage and dressing room, so I had to cross the floor to get there. By the time I made it to the stairs, I was more than a little annoyed because I had had to turn down at least half a dozen dance requests and two requests to go to a private room in the back. I was missing out on a lot of cash, cash that I desperately needed to meet this guy. Whoever he was.

As I climbed the stairs, my nerves started to get the best

of me. I hadn't bothered to put my top back on because I just wanted to get this little meeting over with so I could either pack my things quickly or get back on the floor to make some money while I still could. Now, I wish I had taken the time to at least throw on a t-shirt or robe so that I wasn't meeting the man who was now signing my paychecks with my tits hanging out. Nothing I could do about it now, I suppose.

When I got to the hallway at the top of the stairs, I noticed there were only two doors. One marked *OFFICE* in gold letters. Directly across the hall from the office, was a huge red door with nothing on it. I knocked on the office door first and waited a moment.

Nothing but silence came from the other side of the door. I glanced over my shoulder at the unmarked door. Eve had said the boss wanted to see me in his private suite. Maybe that was the red door.

Tentatively, I turn around, all the little hairs on the back of my neck standing up. I lift my hand to knock on the door, but I hesitate. Years of living on the streets has given me hella good intuition. And right now, all of the warning bells inside my head are going off. Between the way that Eve was acting and this feeling in my gut, I know something is amiss here.

I decide this just isn't worth the risk, and start to turn away, resigning to just go gather my things from my locker and just leave before anyone notices that I'm gone. As I start to turn away, however, a voice booms from the other side of the door.

"Where do you think you are going?"

I flinch at the sound, completely caught off guard, and now more than a little freaked out. "I-I.." I stutter.

"The door is open. Come in," the voice commands.

My hand is shaking as I reach for the knob. My legs want to run, but I know I wouldn't be able to escape as easily as I previously thought. He must have cameras in the hallway or something. How else would he have known I was out here?

I turn the knob slowly, feeling the same tightening of my chest as I did earlier. I swallowed hard as the door opened and I stepped inside. I heard rather than see the door close behind me with a soft click.

The room was dark except for a single floor lamp in the corner next to a large leather couch. My eyes strained to adjust to the dim light, struggling to see anything in the darkness that seemed to engulf all but the small corner. The leather of the couch groaned as a figure leaned forward, placing a glass of amber liquid on a coffee table I hadn't noticed until now.

His large hand made the glass he was just holding look like a toy in comparison. I couldn't see his face, however. He managed to stay shrouded in the darkness as he moved, clearly not as blind as I was by the absence of the light. The only thing I could make out was a faint outline of my companion, whom I could only assume was my new boss. But from that alone, I knew this man was huge.

"You wanted to see me," I said to the man in the darkness, hoping that he didn't hear the sound my racing heart was making in my chest.

The man didn't say a word. Not a sound as he continued to sit there, presumably just staring at me.

Instinctively, I crossed my arms over my chest to hide my naked breasts as I lowered my eyes to the floor.

"Don't you dare cover yourself in front of me," the man in the darkness commanded.

My head snapped up to look in the direction of the voice as recognition washed over me at the sound. My fear and anxiety were suddenly replaced with a burning rage that heated my skin.

No fucking way.

The man reached over and pressed a button on the lamp. The other lights in the room flickered to life, illuminating hard features of the one person I never expected to see.

"You," I said to him through gritted teeth.

The man from the lot just sat there as a sinister smile spread across his smug face.

"Hello, Seraphine."

CHAPTER

FOUR

SAMUEL

She is even sexier than I could have ever imagined she would be under all of those baggy sweats. Even as her pale skin heats and flushes with the rage that is no doubt boiling her blood at the sight of my face, she is the most captivating and alluring human I have ever had the pleasure to lay my eyes upon. She is stunning. Truly an angel brought to life, just as her name would suggest.

"Hello, Seraphine." I can't help the smile that spreads across my face as I speak the name she refused to give me just a few hours previously. Despite popular opinion, I cannot read minds. No one can, except of course, God themself.

"You followed me here, didn't you?" she seethes. "Sick bastard." Her gray-blue eyes bore into me like she is trying to burn me with her gaze alone.

I chuckle as I lean back in my seat again. "No, I assure you I did not follow you here. It was simply a..." I pause and wave my hand in the air as I try to find the right words to describe this unexpected turn of events, "a happy accident."

My words seem to piss her off even more. "Do I look fucking happy?"

I click my tongue and furrow my brow as I reach again for my glass. "Now, that's no way to talk to your new boss, is it?" I chide, knowing exactly how much of an asshole I sound right now.

"After this conversation is over, you can bet your ass that you won't be my boss any longer." She folds her arms across her chest as she speaks, the storm continuing to rage in her eyes.

My smile falls instantly as I grit my teeth in an effort to remain in control. "I told you not to cover yourself," I reminded her with a growl.

"No," she spat back at me.

I rise to my feet in a single movement, never breaking eye contact with her. Even when I reach down and throw, sweeping the contents of the table out of the way, my eyes never leave hers. She barely flinches when the glass of whiskey I had just been drinking shatters against the wall. I close the distance between us in three strides, despite the room being almost double the size of the private rooms reserved for patrons in the back of the main floor. She tilts her head up, also refusing to look away, as I towered over her.

"You will *not* cover yourself in my presence. Ever. Do I make myself clear, Seraphine?" My nostrils flared as I spoke. My voice was filled with barely contained anger at her refusal to do as she was told. Her disobedience was something that would not be tolerated.

She didn't say a single word, but her arms slowly found their sides. She swallowed hard, but her eyes never gave away the fear I could smell on her skin. A twinge of some foreign feeling twisted in my gut. Guilt, maybe? Guilt for frightening her? But why would I feel guilty for that?

After a moment, she lowers her eyes to the floor. For the first time, I notice the way her fingers are trembling slightly. The movement is so small, no mortal would probably even pick up on it. My gut twists again.

I rake my eyes down the length of her body, taking in every detail in all of its glory for the first time. Fucking hell, she is perfect. Her tits are just the right size. I bet if I were to touch them, they would fit perfectly in my hands. Her legs are toned in all the right places. She must have been a dancer for a long time. She is slender, almost too slender, but still has curves in all the right places. And that skin. That beautiful, unmarked, pure white skin. She looks like she bathes in milk every day. There is not even a freckle to be found anywhere on her body. A complete contrast to the deep tan of my tattoo-covered skin.

My dick strains against the zipper of my trousers. Tentatively, I reach towards her, my fingers aching to know if her skin is as soft as it appears to be. She steps back just before my fingers can find their way to her delicate skin, but she doesn't lift her eyes back to mine. I lower my hand, pretending not to notice the way she flinches at the movement.

She's afraid.

Good.

She should be afraid of me. I am, after all, the fucking Devil.

Still, her fear pains me in a way I have never felt before

for anyone, mortal or otherwise. She *should* fear me, but at the same time, I don't want her to.

I turn away from her and retake my seat, picking up my glass before taking a large gulp of the amber liquid. She lifts her eyes slightly in my direction, but not enough to look me in the face. If I am not mistaken, she seems almost surprised that I walked away from her when she retreated. Quite frankly, so am I.

After a moment of silence so loud it echoes from every wall, she lowers her eyes back to the floor. Mine stay fixed on her, though. I note the way her shoulders relax as she turns to leave. Her hand is less shaky as she reaches for the doorknob. I may have respected her unspoken request not to touch her, but I will not be letting her leave and disappear without a trace.

"Where do you think you are going?" The snarl in my tone gave away my annoyance that she was trying to run away from me.

"To finish my shift and then clean out my locker," she said with an indifferent shrug as she turned to face me. "I'd leave right now, but I need the money. So, unfortunately, you're stuck with me for a few hours." She crossed her arms over her chest again, but I didn't correct her this time. My annoyance had shifted to anger, and her disobeying the instructions I had just given her was the least of my concerns at the moment. There was no way I was letting her leave and never return.

"No," I growled, feeling the heat rising in my veins.

"I wasn't asking your permission," she scoffs, her eyes rolling skyward as she speaks.

"You're not quitting," I reiterate, the muscles in my jaw clenching tightly as I try to keep my composure.

"You can't exactly stop me from quitting. And I sure as fuck am not working for *you*." She spins back around on her heel and reaches again for the knob. "I'm going to finish my shift. Every second I spend here is money I am missing out on."

"If you walk out that door, I will personally ensure that every single person on that lot never has a safe place to lay their head at night again."

This gets her attention. She freezes instantly with her hand still on the knob. However, she doesn't turn to face me.

I find myself holding my breath as the seconds tick by agonizingly slowly while I wait for her response to my threat. Her knuckles turn white as she grips the doorknob tighter, the skin on her back flushed with her rage.

"You're bluffing," she says, her trembling voice barely above a whisper, giving her away immediately.

"Try me," I spit out to her back, no longer bothering to contain my frustration at her obstinance. "I am a very powerful man, Seraphine. I don't think you want to find out exactly how powerful."

No one has ever dared to defy me the way this woman has. No one, especially no mortal, has elicited this kind of frustration from me in such a short amount of time. I am both annoyed and aroused at her defiance and will to stick to her guns.

I can tell she is carefully considering my words, letting each one sink in, and trying to figure out if I would truly punish all of those people for her transgression. I would, in the blink of an eye, ensure she does not walk out that door right now. Never in my eternal life have I ever been so willing to go to such lengths, but something about her makes it difficult to let her go so easily.

"Why?" she finally says, her voice cracking with emotion. No doubt she is holding back tears.

"Why what?" I ask with a sigh.

"Why don't you want me to quit? Why do you want to keep me here?"

I answer her question the only way I know how. "Because I'm the Devil, Seraphine," I tell her, a self-satisfied smirk spreading across my lips as I lean back in my seat. "I'll make you a deal."

"A deal with the devil?" she scoffs again, but this time with a confidence I don't think she truly feels any longer. "How fitting."

"It's not the kind of deals I usually make," I chuckle. "Two weeks."

"Two weeks?" she asks as she finally turns again to face me, her nose scrunched in confusion. It's adorably distracting, like a confused little puppy.

"Two weeks," I repeat with a nod. "If you stay, I will extend the time you have to relocate those disgusting vagrants-"

"They are human beings, not disgusting vagrants," she snaps, cutting me off.

I press my lips into a hard line, ignoring her outburst and interruption before I continue. "I will extend the time you have to relocate those *human beings* from my property by two weeks. If you leave, well, as I previously stated, I don't think you want to find out what I am capable of doing to them."

She doesn't speak or move as my words hang heavy in the air. I can see the wheels turning in her pretty little head as she weighs the pros and cons of the ultimatum carefully. She shifts her weights back and forth on her legs, her eyes looking everywhere but at mine. Even her breathing has become more erratic as the reality of what we both know she must do sinks in.

I already know her answer before she even opens her mouth. "Fine. Two weeks. Then, they and I will all be gone." She swallows hard, no doubt feeling as if she has just sold her soul to buy herself and those people a little more time. "And you promise nothing will happen to them?"

I cock my head at her question. "Why do you care so much what happens to them?"

"It doesn't matter," she says quickly, her eyes brimming with her concern for their fate. "Do you promise? Will they be safe there until I can get them relocated?"

I stare at her for a long moment, feeling as if I am seeing something in her that no one else is allowed to see. That she is showing me something she doesn't show anyone. Her vulnerability in this moment breaks something inside of me. She doesn't care what hell I might put her through during her time here. She doesn't care about what might happen to her. Her only concern is them. For whatever reason, she is willing to do this for the chance to save them.

"I swear on all things, holy and unholy, no harm will come to any of them for the duration of your employment with me."

She swallows hard once more and nods, sealing her fate.

We both stare at each other for what feels like an eternity. As someone who has seen eternity begin, even this doesn't feel like an adequate description. Time simply stops as I stare into those eyes, trying to navigate the storm inside them. For a moment, my vision goes red the way it does when I am in my true form. Seraphine gasps and covers her hand with her mouth as her eyes cloud with fear.

"Your eyes..."

"Dance for me," I command, blinking as I look away, trying to keep the monster inside of me from revealing itself.

"But-"

"But what?" I snap, looking back at her when my vision returns to normal and pinning her with my gaze.

"I thought-"

"What did you think?"

"Your eyes. They were-"

"Are you on drugs?"

In an instant, her entire being changes as if I have just slapped her. "No," she snaps.

"Well, you're obviously not hard of hearing. I told you to dance for me."

"No," she repeats.

"I wasn't asking your permission," I smirk, throwing her previous words to me back in her face.

"I would rather be chained naked in front of a bunch of nuns and flogged to death than ever dance for you." And just like that, my little hellcat is back.

"Sounds kinky," I smirk. "I love it."

"Fuck you, asshole."

"Since you offered so nicely," I smirk. "And I've already

told you, it's Samuel. Might want to try to remember that. You'll be screaming it within two weeks."

Her jaw drops open and I would bet my soul, if I had one, that if I were within slapping distance at this moment, my face would have the imprint of her palm on it right now. Instead, she turns away in a huff, stomping out the door in frustration. I bark a laugh before the door slams closed behind her, knowing that she can hear me. I am still laughing when Eve walks in a moment later.

"What was all of that about?" she asks, looking back and forth between me and the door Seraphine had just walked out of.

"A deal," I explain as my laughter dies in my throat as I retrieve another glass from the sidebar.

"A deal?" she repeats, still just as confused as before. "Seraphine never struck me as the type to make a deal with you."

"That's because it wasn't that kind of deal," I elaborate.

"Samuel," she sighs in exasperation as she pinches the bridge of her nose, "please stop speaking in riddles, You know how much I loathe that."

"I will explain my deal with Seraphine as soon as you explain what happened between you and my brother," I smile at her as I down the last of my whiskey.

Eve opens her mouth to speak, but then closes it again before saying anything. Instead, she just purses her lips while avoiding eye contact with me.

I chuckle to myself, shaking my head as I set my now empty glass on the table. "All these years, Eve, and I thought there was nothing I didn't know about you."

"It's nothing you should be concerned about," she explains.

"And neither is my deal with Seraphine," I say with a smile as I pull my phone out of my pocket, opening up the app that allows me to see the feed from the security cameras. I scroll through the various angles until I find the one I am looking for.

On my screen is Seraphine leaning down to talk with some jerkoff in a cheap suit. My smile disappears instantly when I see him hand her a few folded bills before she starts leading him to the back for a private show. My blood boils even more when I notice the way almost every guy in the place is looking at her as she passes by them. One even stops her and slips her some more cash, presumably so he is next in line when she finishes her business with Banker Boy.

My vision goes red again, but I don't give two shits about it. I want nothing more than to unleash all of my wrath on every man who dares to look at her right now. I have felt almost nothing but rage for most of my existence, but this feels different. This is more than anger. This is possession.

Mine.

The word echoes inside my head, only causing my anger to rise as Seraphine disappears into a private room with the man. I could hear Eve talking, but her voice was muted by the sound of the blood rushing in my ears. Visceral rage pounded in my chest. My jaw clenched so tight that I am certain if I could feel physical pain, it would hurt. The only thing I can think of right now is all the ways I want to torture those men for so much as looking at Seraphine.

"Samuel!" Eve said, pulling me from my murderous thoughts.

My eyes snap to hers, then back to the screen. Seraphine and the man are gone, however. I could switch to the feed from inside the room, though I am sure seeing what they are doing will send me over the edge with no chance of coming back.

Replacing my phone in my pocket, I stand and stalk across the room past Eve, yanking the door open so hard I almost rip it from its hinges. "How much does she make a night?" I ask without turning around as I fling the door to my office open, knowing Eve is right on my heels.

"Who? Seraphine?" she asks in bewilderment.

"Yes." My words are clipped and borderline rude, but I don't care right now. The only thing on my mind is making sure that no one lays a hand on what is mine.

"Um," she stammers while I rifle through the top drawer of my desk. "I'm not really sure, to be completely honest. She is probably one of our most popular girls, but I know she is struggling financially."

This gets my attention. "Struggling how?" Perhaps the reason she is so concerned with what happens to the people in that tent city is because she lives there as well.

"I've seen her sneaking fruit from behind the bar a few times. I turned a blind eye to it because it wasn't much and I wasn't going to deny her a free meal if she was hungry. When I spoke to her earlier, she was eating a burger one of the other girls paid for like she hadn't eaten in days. And she is usually late arriving, which I also overlooked, because she walks everywhere. I'm not sure where she lives exactly, but I overheard her on the phone with her landlord explaining that she would be a little late with her rent this month.”

A landlord. Which means she has an apartment at least. So why was she bringing food to those people and making sure they had a safe place to sleep if she was struggling herself? What good was it doing her? Obviously, it wasn’t helping her situation.

“Give her this,” I instruct as I toss three stacks of $100 bills onto the desk.

Eve looks down at the money, then back to me.

“Seraphine is not to do another stage set for the rest of the night. Nor is she to do any dances for anyone, either on the floor or in the back rooms. This should be enough to cover any money she is losing from not being on the floor. Do I make myself clear?”

“Uh, yeah,” Eve says, shaking her head in confusion. “I’ll give her the money and tell her she can just head home for the evening.”

“No!” I bark. “She isn’t allowed to leave, either.”

Eve looks at me, a thousand questions in her brown eyes. She only asks one, however.

“Why is this woman so important to you?”

Holding her gaze, I tell her exactly why.

“I don’t fucking know.”

FIVE

SERAPHINE

ell, that's ten minutes of my life that I'll never get back.

I try to hide my disappointment as I step out of the room after finishing the private dance. To say I was upset would be an understatement. A private dance is fifty bucks per song, of which the club gets ten for its cut. And this asshole decided I wasn't worth a tip since I refused to give him a blow job when he whipped his cock out almost immediately after the song started.

Fuck.

There is no way I am going to be able to feed everyone from the shelter and myself if I don't get some serious tips soon. I could have been on the floor making more than this instead of wasting my time with this guy. Maybe I should have taken him up on his offer.

NO!

I stop that line of thinking dead in its tracks. I'm not going back to that. Stripping is one thing, I'm in control, and I don't have to touch anyone. Going back to turning tricks, no matter the reason, is a slippery slope that I refuse to slide down ever again. I'll come up with the cash some other way.

The guy pushes past me in the hallway, almost knocking me over. He mumbles something as he quickly walks away in frustration, still zipping up his pants after our interaction. I never laid a finger on him, but he still kept his dick out the entire time I danced. I did my best to ignore his pathetic excuse for a cock, and as the dance continued, he became more and more frustrated with the fact that I was not about to drop to my knees for him.

I can't be entirely sure what he said, but I know it wasn't a compliment. He gives me a nasty look over his shoulder, as he faces forward again. He walks into the hard chest of Samuel, his hands in tight fists at his sides and his lips set in a thin hard line.

Samuel acts as if he doesn't even notice the guy as he stumbles backwards and starts cursing loudly, calling Samuel a slew of obscenities. A few of the other customers and dancers turn to see what the commotion is about. Samuel, however, remains oblivious to the man and the onlookers. Instead, his dark brown eyes are locked on mine, pinning me in place.

Samuel's nostrils flare as he stares me down. His perfectly tailored white shirt is unbuttoned at the top and he has removed his tie since our encounter in his private room upstairs. I can see the black lines of a tattoo peeking out of the fabric near his neck. The muscles in his chest rise and fall rapidly with each heavy breath.

I do my best to return the ferocity of his gaze, but inside I am trembling. I tell myself it's out of fear, but as my thighs start to rub together from the ache building between them, I know it's a lie. Even from at least twenty feet away, I can feel him on my skin. Like the way it feels just before lightning is about to strike.

I hate the way my body responds to him almost as much as I hate him. But I have to admit, the way he looks at me turns me on in a way no other man has before. Possessive and protective all at once. A fiery passion mixed with need and rage burns in his eyes. No one has ever looked at me the way he is now.

It feels like an eternity passes before Samuel finally looks down at the guy, who is still spouting off his mouth. The guy, who has to be at least a foot shorter and a hundred pounds lighter, seems completely unbothered by the size difference between himself and Samuel. Samuel's eyes reluctantly leave mine, shifting to a look of cold fury as he glares down at the asshole.

The guy was a regular, though I never bothered to learn his name. I made it a point to not learn the names of the guys who frequented the club. Even after only being here for a few weeks, I noticed which ones were here most every night. Learning their names seemed too personal to me. Instead, I gave the frequent flyers nicknames that I would associate with something about them to keep them straight in my head. A way of being personal without being personal. This guy worked in a chocolate factory so I called him Sweets.

His face suddenly turns grim as Sweets suddenly realizes

that he may have made a grave mistake in talking to Samuel like that. All of the color drains from his face as the curse he was about to say dies on his lips. Samuel snaps his fingers and security appears from the shadows of the wings. The two guards, whose names escape my foggy brain at the moment, grab Sweets by the arm and escort him upstairs. Sweets begins to protest, then beg to be released, promising he will leave and not return. The guards ignore his request as they continue what I can only describe as a death march to the second floor.

Samuel watches as the man is led away. His strained muscles twitch under his expensive shirt. With his head turned like this, I can clearly see the veins in his neck like pythons coiled around a thick tree trunk.

Why the fuck are they not kicking him out? I think to myself as the men disappear behind the door at the top of the stairs.

Samuel snaps his head around, returning his attention to me. His expression is not the same as before, however. His eyes are cold and hard as they bore into mine. The fire that was just there snuffed out and replaced with ice. A chisel races down my spine. The room seems to drop at least twenty degrees as he brings his eyes back to meet mine. I never knew eyes so dark could be so cold.

His lips curl as he bares his teeth in a menacing snarl. His eyes rake over my bare skin, pausing for the briefest of moments at my tits before finishing their journey downward. There is a faint red mark on my nipple where Sweets tried to grab me at some point and I can feel the bruise forming on my ass from the smack that caused me to finally cut the dance short.

The music is pounding, but I am certain I can hear Samuel growl even above the pulsing beat. The sound reverberates across my sensitive skin, causing goosebumps to bloom across my chest. This seems to only make Samuel more angry.

But why? Why is he so pissed at me? I didn't do anything wrong. And I have the lack of tips to prove it. I clutch the money in my fist, feeling my skin tingle and heat. This time, for an entirely different reason than it had a few moments ago. How dare he look at me like that! Like I'm some kind of whore!

A wave of shame fuels my sudden rage. I swallow the memories of my past down before they have a chance to choke me. I'm not that person anymore. And he has no right to look at me as if I am.

With the most disrespectful smirk I can muster, I lift my hand and flip him off before turning away to stomp off. Well, as best I can in six-inch heels. I flip my hair over my shoulder without looking back as a final insult.

I can already feel her coming up behind me as I push open the door to the dressing room. "Seraphine," Eve calls after me, her bare feet padding against the painted concrete floor as she follows me in.

"Save it, Eve," I snap, yanking the door to my locker open. I had tossed my top in my locker before I went upstairs earlier. I grabbed it, tying it back on more forcefully than I probably should, considering how cheap and worn the material is. Shoving the cash in my bag, I continue without bothering to look at her. "You can go tell your boss that I'm not leaving. Our deal is still intact. I just need to cool off for a second before I head back out on the floor."

"Yeah, about that," she says sheepishly, twirling a piece of hair around her finger and looking anywhere but at me.

I spin around on my heel to face her. "Is he *firing* me?!" I shriek in bewilderment.

"No!" She exclaims. She closes her eyes for a moment and takes a deep breath, almost as if she is trying to calm herself and gather her thoughts. "No, it's nothing like that."

"Good," I sigh, running my fingers through my hair as I feel myself starting to calm down as well. I may be pissed, but I need this job.

"Buuuutttt..." she continues.

"But what?" A million scenarios run through my head. Is he sending me home for the night? Would that count as breaking our deal if he does? After the house cut of what I have made so far tonight, I'm certain I would have to choose between buying food or getting my phone cut back on. Do I have anything left at my apartment that I can pawn or sell?

"But, you can't go back on the floor tonight." She says the words in a rush, but at least she looks at me when she says them.

"What?" I ask, crossing my arms over my chest and scrunching my nose in confusion. I am not completely sure what she means by this. "I have to go back on the floor. I need the money and I have two more stage sets later."

"Jenna is going to do your stage sets," she tells me, as if that somehow explains everything. Quite the opposite, though.

"Are you serious?" I ask, even more confused than before. "Why can't I go back out there?" The knot that had been forming in my chest presses down further on my lungs. With my arms still crossed, I discreetly rub my fist in tiny circles on my sternum to try to lessen the tightness. *Just breathe, Seraphine,* I tell myself. I can't risk a panic attack right now.

"It's..I-I...we..." she stammers.

Warning bells start going off inside my head. Eve is the most confident woman I have ever met in my life. I've never seen her this nervous before. Something is most definitely off, and everything inside of me is screaming that I need to run away. Now.

I take a cautious step backwards, trying to create a little more distance between Eve and myself. If experience has taught me anything, it's that space is your friend when someone starts acting as much out of the ordinary as she is now. As I am trying to move away subtly, I notice something in Eve's hand.

No.

Not something. *Somethings.*

"Why do you have those stacks in your hand, Eve?" My question comes out with a slight edge of fear.

She looks down at the money in her hand as if she had forgotten it was even there to begin with. "It's, um," she starts, still looking down at the cash, like she wasn't sure herself why she was holding what had to be at least a couple grand.

She suddenly thrusts her hand outward towards me, making me recoil slightly before regaining my composure.

"This is for you," she says very matter-of-factly, shaking the stacks of cash at me.

I look at her hand, then back at her, I don't dare reach for the money, even though my mind is already running the numbers at exactly what I could do with it. There is no way that kind of cash doesn't come with some kind of strings attached to it.

"What's the catch?" I ask flatly with more than a little skepticism in my voice.

"There isn't one." She seems to have found her lost confidence as she speaks. I'm still not buying it, though.

"I learned a long time ago, Eve, that nothing in this world comes without strings attached."

She releases a heavy sigh, but doesn't lower her arm. "All I know is someone gave me this and told me to give it to you. In exchange, you are to not go back on the floor."

"So what am I supposed to do? Just wait for them in one of the private rooms?"

"Yes!" she exclaims with a little too much excitement. "Yes, you are to wait for them in the VIP room."

I stare at the money. Whoever is willing to pay this much for a private dance is definitely going to expect more than a three minute song and a no touching policy. On the other hand, that kind of money would solve a lot of problems for me—rent, food, phone. Hell, I may even be able to get a bus pass if there is enough left over. But are all of those things really worth going back to that life?

"No."

My response obviously catches Eve off guard. "N-No?" she stutters, clearly thinking she must have misheard me.

"No," I repeat. "I know what that kind of money means. So tell whoever it is, thanks but no thanks."

"What it means?" she says, repeating my words as if she is still trying to wrap her head around my rejection.

"Yeah. The *extra* services that will be expected if I take the money," I explain, emphasizing the word extra so it is clear to her what I am trying to say.

Eve throws her head back and laughs, finally lowering her arm. "Oh, hell no!" she laughs. "Seraphine, I would never put you in that kind of position," she explains, taking a step forward and placing what is supposed to be a reassuring hand on my shoulder. I try to hide the way my muscles instinctively tighten at the contact. Still haven't been able to get past being touched. Fortunately, Eve notices my micro reaction and removes her hand without calling attention to it. "I know what you're thinking, but I assure you it isn't like that."

"Then what is it like?"

"Someone would just prefer it if you would wait for them in the private room. And they are willing to pay for you to do so. That's all."

Something still feels off. "So they just want me to wait for them? Wait for how long?"

"Now, that, I am not sure. They did not specify."

"Who is the customer? Is it one of the regulars?" I scan my memory for any of the regulars I've met for anyone who seems like the type to be able to afford such a request, but no one jumps out as a possible suspect.

"The client...wishes to remain anonymous." Eve twists a piece of hair around her finger again, something I am learning is a tell of her when she is nervous.

More questions than answers run through my head, making me a little dizzy. But also, a little curious. To say I trust Eve when she says nothing more is expected of me would be a bit of an overstatement. Trust is not a word I use. Ever. This time, however, I almost feel like I should trust her.

My eyes drop down to the money still in her hand. "How much is he paying?"

"Uhhhhhh," Eve says, looking down at the stacks wrapped in little paper bands. Fresh from the bank, it would appear. "Looks like three grand."

Three thousand dollars to sit and wait for someone. Possibly dance for a few minutes for them. No expectations of anything else. I've done a lot more for a lot less.

"Tell the mystery man I'll be waiting for him in VIP One." The tightness in my chest returns full force, forcing all the air from my lungs in a rush as I speak.

"Oh, thank g-" Eve stops before finishing the word. I don't think she realizes the way her jaw clenches, but I see it. I know she isn't exactly religious, but she suddenly looks down right angry at herself for almost uttering the word. A split second later, she shakes her head and her momentary rage is gone. "I'll let him know."

"Let him know one more thing, too," I say as Eve starts to turn to walk away.

"What's that, sweetie?"

"Tell him, he lays so much as a fucking finger on me, I'll rip his cock off and feed it to him."

Eve blinks a few times as my threat sinks in. Then she does something that takes me completely off guard. She smiles. Not a fake, I'm-just-smiling-to-hide-my-discomfort smile. This is a genuine, knowing smile.

"I think I understand now," she says, her tone like a mother speaking lovingly to her child.

"Understand what?"

Her smile widens, touching her kind eyes. "I understand now why you're so important to him."

CHAPTER

SIX

SAMUEL

I've grown accustomed to sleep since my fall from the Heavens. It is one of the few things I have found pleasure in during my exile. So it is safe to say I am more than a little fucking pissed off that I am still lying here, staring up at the ceiling, as the birds outside my window begin their insufferable chirping.

I didn't sleep that night after the incident with a regular at Eden. In fact, I haven't slept at all in the three days since then. Instead, I have spent my nights lying awake, thinking of that woman. That goddamn woman. Even when I am not obsessively watching her every movement on the cameras as she sits in the VIP room each night, waiting for a client who never comes, I still can't escape her. How fucking pathetic.

As the first rays of light from the rising sun start to peek around the edges of my curtains, I feel myself finally starting to drift off to sleep. Within seconds, I am pulled into a deep slumber. No doubt from the sheer exhaustion of being awake for the last 72 hours. But my dreams are still consumed by her.

Visions of her slender frame dance in my head. Her pale skin. Her ocean blue eyes. Those perfect fucking tits. The dream is so real, I can feel her moving on top of me as she rides my cock. I can feel each time her tight pussy squeezes me as her body rocks back and forth. Hell, I can even smell the saltiness of her skin as the sweat beads on her skin, reminding me of the smell of the ocean after the rain. Even the sweet sounds of the moans falling from her lips when she comes echo in my ears.

I sat upright with a jolt, my skin sticky with sweat. Violently, I kick the black sheets to the floor as if they have personally offended me. Free from the constraints of the bedding, my cock stands at full attention. It pulsates, a bead of precum glistening in the faint light of the morning sun. I always sleep naked, not ashamed in the least of my mortal form. I've never given two shits about who sees me in all my human glory. I knew what I looked like, and I knew that I looked good. Now, however, as I watch my dick twitch with a need for release, I hate every single molecule of this body.

The physical manifestation of the power this woman has over me is an affront to my very being. It would seem I cannot escape it, even in my dreams. A frustrated growl rumbles in my chest as I lower myself back down on the pillows. I scrub my face with one hand as the other slides down my torso. I grip the shaft of my cock to the point of mortal pain, despite feeling nothing but unadulterated rage at myself for what I am about to do.

I want nothing more than to rip my betraying cock from my body. Never, in all this time, have I ever jerked off before. I've never had to. There has always been more than enough willing pussy around to keep me satisfied. Which makes my blood boil even more as my grip starts to loosen and my hand starts to move up and down the length of my dick.

For a moment, I contemplate stopping. One call, and I could have any number of beings at my door; all of them willing and able to take every ounce of frustration I needed to release. Lilith has been all but begging for a good fuck for a while now. One call, and I know she would be here, letting me do every unholy thing I can imagine to her. The thought is fleeting, though. Because I know it wouldn't matter. I know, no matter who I call, who I ravage, who I fuck into oblivion, there is only one creature who can sate my lust now.

"Samuel." Seraphine's breathless whimpering of my name is so real, I can feel her lips as they brush against my ear. She sounds so needy. Is she? Wherever she is right now, does this all-consuming need torture her as well?

My hand continues to move at a torturously slow pace, mimicking the image in my head of Seraphine riding me. I squeeze myself in the same way I know her tight cunt would. My breath starts coming in short, ragged pants as my eyes roll in the back of my head. The smell of her sex fills my nostrils. The precum leaks from my tip, rolling down my shaft and lubing my hand as I start stroking myself faster.

My teeth grind as I fight my pending release. I don't want to come. Not like this. I want to come buried deep in her perfect little pussy. I hate the thought of wasting a drop by spilling myself all over my expensive sheets. But fighting this is like fighting the entirety of the Heavenly Host all over again. I have no chance of winning this battle, but that doesn't stop me from trying.

The blood rushes in my ears, sounding like waves crashing angrily against the rocks. I feel her delicate skin on mine. The sensation is as real as the breath filling my lungs. In my head, her hips buck wildly as she rides me. My hand matches her movements, increasing my tempo along with hers. I can see those perfect tits of hers as they bounce. The diamond hard peaks beg to be pinched. I stop myself before actually reaching out to touch the woman on top of me, who isn't really there at all.

Sweat beads across my burning skin. My hand moves faster and faster as I lose my inner battle with my release. In my head, Seraphine throws her head back in ecstasy, on the cusp of her own release. My heart races. My human heart, at least. The jury is still out on if I have anything capable of emotion.

I can almost feel her nails digging into my chest. The feeling causes my bitter growls to shift to long, husky moans. The familiar sensation of release starts to crawl up my spine. I squeeze my shaft hard in a desperate attempt to stave off the eruption.

"Come with me, Samuel," I hear her breathe. Just the sound of her voice, almost pleading with me to come, almost causes me to blow my load on the spot. Rage and desire swirl in my blood, both trying to overtake the other. *"Please,"* she begs again.

"No!" I audibly grit out between clenched teeth as my hand continues to move. Every muscle in my body is strained tight as a tripwire. My balls draw up, aching for release, but I refuse to let go.

"Samuel, I can't-" she begs. I can feel the ghost of her touch; her legs trembling as she chases her own release.

I feel her walls tighten around me, pushing out the little voice in my head reminding me that it's just my hand. *"I can't hold-"* Her voice cracks under the strain of holding herself back. I don't want to come. Coming feels like defeat right now. And I will not be defeated by her.

"Samuel, please!"

With her final plea, I am undone. I don't just fall over the edge, I jump, erupting in a thunderous explosion of pleasure. The force of my climax vibrates throughout my entire body, making the bed shake with the magnitude. My throat goes numb, my voice straining as I roar my release. The sound is deafening, even to my ears. Thick, white ropes of cum cover my sheets, thighs, and lower abdomen. Never have I experienced anything like this in all my eternal years.

The weight of what just happened crashes down on me as my cock starts to soften in my hand. My erratic breathing slowly starts to return to normal, the euphoria of the orgasm quickly fading. The sweat on my skin starts drying, sending a cold shiver across my cooling skin.

Rage blossoms anew in my chest. This woman, without even knowing it, without even fucking being here, has done this to me. She led me to the very edge of oblivion. And I willingly followed her over the edge, not knowing what awaited me at the bottom was my own destruction. It is in this moment, alone in my bedroom and covered in the remnants of the power she wields over me, I realize exactly how fucked I truly am.

This woman could go anywhere, Heaven, Hell, it doesn't matter, and I would blindly follow her. Without even knowing it, this fucking mortal has brought the Devil himself to his goddamn knees.

And, for that, we are both damned.

After my release, I called for housekeeping to come and clean up the mess I had made on the bed while I took a shower. My body was bone tired, and I don't even remember climbing back under the sheets. I simply passed out, though my sleep was restless after my realization.

When I finally awoke a few hours later, a new sense of purpose washed over me. I was not going to let this mortal creature pull me down into the depths of a Hell even I did not want to go. However, I was not ready to relinquish her to anyone else, either. She would never know it, but she would forever be mine, even if I was never hers.

At the club, when she was safely tucked away from prying eyes in the VIP room, I had watched her on the cameras. I followed her home every night after closing. I observed her interactions with those people at the vacant lot before she would start her shift every day. There was hardly a time since I first laid eyes on her that she was out of my sight.

Stalking has always been a strong suit of mine. There wasn't much I couldn't learn about someone from watching them in the shadows. It made acquiring their soul much easier when I knew exactly what to offer them without them even having to ask. Seraphine was no different.

As I selected my suit from the closet and began getting dressed for the day, I recalled what I had observed over the last few days. I would say her apartment was a shithole, but that would be an insult to shitholes. I also learned that my original concerns that she wasn't eating enough were right. She spends most of her money on those people. The why still baffles me, though. She's behind on her rent, starving herself, and two steps away from homelessness herself. Why does she give two shits about them? I have a feeling, if I find the answer to that question, I will find a way to keep her close but still at a safe distance.

After dressing, I walk out of my obscenely large closet and back into the main bedroom. My lip curls in disgust at the sight of the bed. Even with fresh sheets, I can still smell myself all over it. Normally, the fresh smell of sex intoxicates me. This time, however, it offends me on a personal level. I all but growl at the betraying piece of furniture as I yank the bedroom door open and step out into the hallway, slamming the door behind me so hard, I hear the wood crack.

"Have someone remove that bed and all the linens," I snap at Drakin, who is waiting for me at his normal post outside my door. "I want them burned and replaced before I get back tonight."

His steps falter slightly at my request, but he regains himself just as quickly. "The entire bed, sir?" he asks, my request obviously catching him more than a little off guard. Drakin was the first to follow me in my rebelion. He's been my right hand longer than time can measure. In all that time, however, I've never seen him caught off guard. Especially not for something as simple as replacing a bed. But I ignore his reaction for now.

"Yes," I confirm with a snarl. "The entire thing. Sheets, comforter, all of it. Mattress too. I want it all removed. And make sure it is not just dumped." I don't want that thing to be found in a dumpster and salvaged by some crackhead looking for free shit. I want all traces of what I did destroyed. Maybe then, I will be able to get some goddamn peace.

"Yes, sir," he nods.

Drakin knows better than to question me further about this. He may not understand the reason behind it, but he doesn't press the issue. Another reason I have trusted him as long as I have.

"Did you contact the local police as I requested?"

"Yes, sir," he answers, his voice returning to its normal tone. He is no doubt thankful and relieved to have the conversation back on business he knows about rather than obscure requests he has to guess at.

"And?" I ask, stabbing the call button on the elevator with a little more force than is necessary.

"They are waiting for your call." The elevator dings its arrival and we step inside. Drakin presses the button for the garage as the doors slide closed. "The chief assures me it would take no more than ten minutes for their officers to arrive at the lot from the time of the call. He is being very cooperative."

"Perfect." He is being cooperative because he values his life. I abhor violence unless it is absolutely required.

However, I am still the Devil. And my reputation definitely precedes me.

"He also assured me that he can have all of the squatters removed and relocated out of town as soon as *humanly* possible." Drakin chuckles at his little joke, but then clears his throat and goes silent when he realizes I am not laughing.

Thoughts race through my head; a jumbled mess of conflicting decisions. I want those people off of my land. I *need* them off of my land. If we don't start construction soon, there is no way we will be able to open on time. Delaying the opening will cost me a lot of money. Under normal circumstances, I wouldn't give a fuck. I would make the call, have those people loaded onto a bus, and dump them out in the middle of the desert somewhere without a second thought. This, however, is not normal circumstances.

I know if I just load these people onto a bus and ship them off somewhere, Seraphine will never forgive me. Which may be for the best. Hell, it would be for the best. She needs to stay as far away from me as possible, for her own good. But I'm too much of a selfish bastard to ever let that happen.

My muscles in my neck spasm, twitching with frustration under my skin. This shouldn't be a hard choice. I should make the call. I should do what I need to and to Hell with Seraphine or anyone else who might get in the way. I should not be giving this a second thought. Instead, I find myself second guessing something I should not be giving a single solitary fuck about. These people mean nothing to me.

But her.

I still don't understand exactly what I feel for her. I don't even know if I feel anything at all, or if this is just some kind of twisted lust thing. Of all people, I should know the difference, yet here we are. Here I am. And I fucking hate it here.

I need to fuck this bitch out of my system and soon. The longer I go without burying my cock in her sweet pussy, the deeper I slip under her intoxicating spell. The thought of losing myself to this sets my teeth on edge. The faster I get her sexy little body under mine, the faster I can get her out of my fucking head.

"Sir?" Drakin says, pulling me from my conflicting thoughts.

"What?" My tone has an edge to it, but I don't bother with an empty apology.

"Should I call them now?"

I open my mouth to answer him, but close it again without a word. Then, a lightbulb goes off in my head. A solution that would give me what I want, in every way. I'm almost mad at myself for not seeing the answer sooner.

"Yes," I instruct him, a twisted smirk curling at the corners of my mouth as the elevator doors slide open. "Tell the chief to have his men meet us at the lot in ten minutes."

SEVEN

SERAPHINE

The sheets stick to my sweat covered skin like gum stuck to the bottom of your shoe. They cling uncomfortably to me and refuse to let go no matter which way I roll in my bed. Of course, I use the term "bed" loosely. It's really just two worn out mattresses stacked in the only available corner of my apartment.

I kick the sheets off for the millionth time tonight. The cool air from my open window does little to cool me off. Goosebumps break out across my skin, causing me to pull the sheets up once again. It's the same pattern I've repeated all night. Every night for the past three nights, actually. Sweat. Sticky. Sheets. Goosebumps. Sheets. Throwing my arm over my eyes, I finally just give up. The sun is already starting to filter into the room through the holes in my curtain anyway. Not much use trying to sleep now.

I grumble to myself, making a mental note to sew a few more patches into those curtains next chance I get, and crawl out of bed. The concrete floor is ice cold, despite it being late summer. My eyes burn with exhaustion. I haven't had more than a few minutes of sleep at a time since the other night. But I'm too tired to focus on that right now.

My apartment is small, to say the very least. But it's better than I am used to. And it was all I could afford after getting out of the hospital. It'll do for now. Until I can figure out a better solution.

My feet drag across the cold floor, my legs feeling like someone filled them with cement during the night. Luckily, one of the perks of having a small place is it doesn't take long to get where you are going. The "kitchen", if you can even call it that, is nothing more than a mini fridge with two rolling carts on either side of it, and a microwave. I had a single burner hotplate, but had to get rid of it. Damn thing kept tripping the breakers and overwhelming the shitting wiring in this place. There isn't even a sink for dishes, not that I have any anyway. Just an old and heavily stained coffee mug that I got at the thrift store. It's easy enough to rinse out in the bathroom sink, though, when I'm done with it.

I grab the mug off of the bent nail above the microwave. Best hook I've ever owned, if I'm being honest. Even with the rest of this place basically crumbling around me, that nail has never so much as wiggled. I grab the instant coffee and a bottle of water out of the fridge. It's the only place I can store what little food I have so that the mice and roaches don't get in it.

I pour the water into the mug and pop it in the microwave to heat up. The process can take anywhere from five to ten minutes, depending on what mood my shitty little microwave wants to be in today. While I wait, I decide

I may as well take a shower to wash the sweat that has now dried to my skin.

The bathroom is exactly what you would expect, given the state of the rest of the

apartment. It's basically two pieces of cheap plywood held up by L-brackets in the floor and ceiling with a crudely cut out rectangle where the door should be. The shower is just a nozzle connected to the sink and draped over a bar with a drain cut into the floor. I'm not even entirely certain the drain is actually attached to any pipes. And, since there is no actual door, I'm pretty much on full display to anyone else who may be visiting at the time. Not that I ever have anyone over.

I jiggle the knob on the sink and the faucet spurts and sputters to life. After the initial brown colored liquid that always comes out when I first turn it on starts to run clear, I turn the other knob to divert the water to the shower. It usually heats up fairly quickly, which was a bit of a surprise to me the first time I showered here, but I don't even wait this time. I strip out of the white tank top and panties I am wearing and toss them just past the threshold of the bathroom before stepping under the still cold spray.

I close my eyes as I let the water wash over my face. My tense muscles slowly start to relax as the water gradually warms. A small sigh releases from my lips. I hadn't realized just how worked up I had gotten from the lack of sleep. But was my sudden bout of insomnia really to blame for all of this tension? A voice in my head that I have been trying to ignore for the past three days tells me no, it isn't.

I grab the near-empty bottle of shampoo from the floor next to my feet and squeeze some in my hand. As I work the lather throughout my hair, I go over what all I need to get done today before heading to the club for my shift. It's nothing more than a half assed attempt to block out the thoughts I can already feel seeping into my mind, but I try not to focus on that. Try not to focus on him.

The money Eve has given me each night from my secret admirer has been a Godsend. Before that first night, I was three months behind on my rent. It was a miracle my bitch of a landlady hadn't served me with an eviction notice already. I had been dodging her for weeks, trying to come up with a solution to my rent situation before she had the chance to kick me out. The timing of this guy, whoever he was, coming along couldn't have been any better.

After stopping by the complex's office this morning, I was going to go grab some supplies for everyone at the lot. When I was there yesterday, I noticed there were more people than when I originally helped move everyone there from the shelter. More people meant more food, more water, more everything. The scraps I had been dropping off were no longer going to be enough to go around. But with this money, I could make sure everyone had something to eat and maybe a few little extras. Hell, I might even have enough left over to get my cell phone turned back on and a bus pass so I didn't have to walk to work anymore. I wasn't getting my hopes up, however.

As I rinsed the suds from my hair, my thoughts finally found their way back to the one person I was actively trying to avoid thinking of. *Samuel.* Why couldn't I get that asshole out of my fucking head? And why was I actually glad that I couldn't?

Ever since first meeting him at the lot, I've felt this...

electricity. And I hate it. I hate him. I hate everything he stands for. I hate that he holds the fate of so many people I care about in his hands. Most of all, I hate the way my body reacts when I see him.

I've actually done a pretty good job of avoiding him since that first night. That hasn't stopped this feeling, though. Every time I set foot in the club, I can feel his eyes on me. But it's silly to think a man like him is up in his office wasting his time watching me on the security cameras. Plus, I haven't even danced since that first night we met. I've been tucked away in the VIP room, sitting there waiting for some mystery client that never shows.

I'm not exactly complaining about that part. The past few nights, as soon as I get to the club, Eve has met me with a stack of cash and instructions to go wait in VIP. I'm not sure who it is that has paid so much to not spend any time with me, but I am definitely not complaining either.

The first night, I was nervous. Despite what Eve said about it not being that kind of interaction, I was still fairly certain that whomever it was, would likely be expecting more than a dance for the amount of money they were paying. I made a promise to myself that I would never go back to selling my body again, no matter what. But this would have been different. It would mean I could get enough cash to really help everyone who had been affected when the shelter got closed down. It wouldn't be for selfish reasons, like it had been in the past. So, what harm could it do if I just maybe went down on the guy, whoever he was, if it was for a good cause?

Luckily, I never had to answer that question. No one ever showed that night. Or the next night. Or last night.

From the moment I walked into VIP, the only person I would see was Eve when she would bring me some food. Good food, too. Not the cheap snacks we served at the bar, but charcuterie boards with expensive cheeses, thinly sliced meats, and fresh fruits. Last night, she even brought me a book to help pass the time. Oddly enough, it was a book I had mentioned to her a couple weeks ago that I had been wanting to read. I spent my entire shift lounging on the couch, reading my new book, and grazing the board while I sipped the best sparkling water I had ever tasted.

I pinch the bridge of my nose, trying to force the image of Samuel watching me as I sat there reading last night. It's crazy to think of. Why would he waste his time watching me? After the disgusted look he gave me when he saw me walking out of a private room with Sweets, it's pretty obvious how he sees me.

Whore.

The word echoes in my ears, as if someone was right behind me, screaming it over and over again. I cover my ears to block out the imaginary sound. The warm water washes over my skin, mixing with my tears as they burn streaks down my cheeks. My heart races behind my ribcage, the sound thundering in my ears and blocking out every other sound. Panic catches in my throat, choking me and stealing my breath. My legs feel like warm, watered-down jello, threatening to buckle from the weight of my own body. My jaw clenches so tightly that it hurts as I try desperately to keep the memories of my life before from taking over.

Just as I feel the weight of my past taking over, something stops me from falling. It startles me at first. I gasp, nearly jumping out of my skin in shock, at the feeling of two strong arms snaking their way around my waist. My eyes fly open as I spin around, almost slipping and falling on the wet tile. But there is nothing there. No intruder, no ghost, no nothing.

I release a heavy sigh of relief, turning back under the hot spray to finish rinsing myself off. Then, the arms slide around me again. This time, however, I don't react. I freeze in place, terrified about what is happening.

"Seraphine," a voice said in a hoarse whisper, the sound so close I could feel his breath against my skin.

Samuel.

I slowly opened my eyes again, looking down and halfway expecting to see his tattooed covered arms wrapped around me. But there was nothing there. I touched the place on my abdomen where I could clearly feel his touch, but all I felt was my own skin.

"Close your eyes, woman," his voice rasped in my ear.

"No," I reply audibly. Even in my own imagination, I refuse to give into him without a fight.

His responding growl sends a shiver down my spine. *"So defiant,"* he grits out in a low rumble in my ear. A sharp intake of air fills my lungs as I swear I can feel his teeth nip my collarbone. *"Close your fucking eyes."*

I open my mouth to deny his request again, but close it again without a word. Slowly, I acquiesce and close my eyes. A calm washes over me like the water from the showerhead. I feel my heart rate starting to slow, and my body stops trembling. Even though I know it's not real, I can feel his chest against my bare back. The corners of my mouth twitch up in a small smile as I feel his chest hair tickling my skin.

The feeling of his skin against mine, real or not, both soothes and enrages me. With my eyes closed, I can see him perfectly in my head. I can see the look of pure disgust he gave me that night when he saw me leaving the private room. The way he snarled at my nakedness and glared at me with ice cold fire in his eyes.

I see the way he first looked at me that day at the lot. His contemptuous judgment of myself and everyone as I handed out food. When he grabbed me that day, I know he wanted to hit me. I could see it in his eyes. It's the same look I've seen a hundred times. The fact that he stopped himself doesn't change the fact that he thought about it.

However, I can also see clearly in my head the way he looked at me that night in his private room. The way his eyes devoured every inch of my body. The way he refused to allow me to cover myself. The way he looked like he wanted to fuck the soul out of me right then and there.

I rub my thighs together, feeling the familiar ache starting to build between my legs. The ghost-like feeling of Samuel's arms once again wraps around my waist. This time, though, I keep my eyes closed so they don't disappear.

I can feel his large hand covering mine. His fingers tangle with mine as he guides my hand lower. *"Touch yourself for me, woman."* His voice is commanding, even if it isn't real. I push back against his guidance, silently disobeying his request. But how do you resist something your own body wants?

Yes, I feel Samuel's body behind mine. I can even feel his cock stiffening as it nestles and rests between the cheeks of my ass. Hell, I can even feel him breathing against the side of my neck. But it's not real. He isn't the one sliding my hand lower and lower down my abdomen. I am the one doing it. So, is it really giving in if I am the one in control to begin with?

My head is spinning and clouded from exhaustion and lust. I know I am not thinking straight. I know I am making a mistake doing this. I also know that I just don't give a fuck right now.

I slip my fingers between my legs, exploring my own wetness as if I have never felt it before. *"That's it,"* he hisses, subconsciously pushing my fingers inside me. *"Show me how you make yourself come."*

A soft moan escapes my lips as my fingers move inside me. Even though it is my hand, I feel Samuel guiding my every move. It's erotic and heady and unlike anything I have ever felt before. I both love and hate the sensation.

My free hand slides up my wet skin, cupping my heavy breast. I bite down hard on my bottom lip when I feel his hands guiding mine to pinch my own nipple.

My legs start to feel weak again, though this time for an entirely different reason. My breath comes in short pants, matching the increasing tempo of my fingers. I am on the precipice of a cliff, and I am not sure I want to go over it. The pressure inside me is building, pushing me higher and higher with no end in sight.

"You better fucking come, woman," I hear Samuel growl, his voice strained, as if he is holding back his own orgasm.

"Not on your life," I chuckle, already knowing I am fighting a losing battle with myself.

"Fucking obstinant, disobedient woman," he snarls.

I laugh again, pushing my ass against his hard cock and feeling every inch of his length pulsating with need to release. It's not real. I know it's not real. That doesn't stop me from fighting him at every opportunity. Even if it is all in my head, he will never have this power over me.

I feel his hand grip mine even harder, all but forcing me to go deeper inside myself. My thumb circles my clit without actually touching it. It's blissful torture of the best kind. Neither of us wanting to be the first to let go. Neither of us willing to give that power to the other. Just when I think I have the upper hand, and he will be the first to break, I feel his teeth sink into my skin at the same time my thumb finally finds my clit.

To say I explode would be an understatement and an insult. My vision blurs, and I honestly feel as if I am about to pass out with the force of my orgasm. Nothing in my life has ever felt as good as this. Nothing in my life has ever felt as real.

My senses slowly start to return to me as I slide my back down the tile to sit on the floor of the shower. The water is starting to go cold, causing my skin to break out in a fresh wave of goosebumps. My breathing is still ragged while my heart continues to pound in my chest. The reality of what just happens starts to creep into my head as the remnants of Samuel's touch fades from my overly sensitive skin.

The sound of the microwave beeping is the final snap back to reality for me. *Oh, God.* Did I really just do what I think I just did? Did I really just come from the mere thought of Samuel touching me? I try to ignore the voice inside my head laughing at me, calling me a whore all over again, but it's too loud to block it out this time. And this time, no one comes to silence it.

EIGHT

The rest of the morning was spent in a numb sort of autopilot. After what happened in the shower, I shut down completely. How could I let myself do that? How could he have that kind of control over me? I swore to myself I would never let anyone hold that kind of power over my body ever again. Even the thought of what I let happen makes my blood boil.

I push the memory of what I did to the back of my mind as I round the corner of the sidewalk on my way to deliver today's meals. I don't want to show up on the lot with this hanging over my head. And it's not like I can take it back now. What's done is done, and I am just going to have to accept it, move on, and make sure I never let something like that ever happen again.

It did feel good, though. Great, actually. Better than great. I haven't made myself come like that in a very long time, if ever. Since leaving the hospital a few months ago, masturbating hasn't exactly been one of my top priorities. Plus, with being around horny men all night at Eden and having to pretend to be as horny as they are, I haven't really had much of a reason to get turned on lately. Why, though, did it have to be the thought of *him* to get me so hot and bothered?

As I round the last corner and the lot comes into view, all thought about what happened in the shower this morning evaporates from my brain. I stop dead in my tracks. At least a dozen police cruisers and two prison transport buses are blocking off the street in front of the lot. More than twenty cops in uniform are scattered across the lot, rounding everyone up and herding them onto the buses. Another group of cops are disassembling some of the tents and gathering up the bags and belongings of everyone who had been staying here, shoving everything into black plastic bags and tossing them aside in a giant pile. When my brain finally catches up to what my eyes are seeing, I drop the grocery bags I was carrying and start sprinting towards the crowd.

"Hey!" I scream as I approach at full speed. "Stop! You can't do that!" One of the cops catches me around the waist. I try to twist out of his grip, pushing at his chest while he manhandles me like a fucking ragdoll. "What the fuck do you think you are doing?" I yell at no one in particular.

"Calm down, sweetie," the one who has a hold on me says while pulling me backwards.

"I'm not your fucking sweetie, you goddamn jackass!" I spit at him, still fighting to get out his grip. "Let me the fuck go!"

The cop looks me up and down, his eyes glossing over

with disgust and knowing. "Call down, you little slut, or I'll-"

"Or you'll what?" I scream in his face, cutting him off mid sentence.

He leans down so close I can smell his rancid breath as he speaks. "Or I'll take you behind that wall over there and show you what we do with your kind around here."

I open my mouth to say something, but I don't get the chance.

"Take your fucking hands off of her."

The voice is deep, but not raised. It doesn't need to be. He conveys everything he needs to with his tone alone. I continue to struggle as the cop just stares behind me.

I can't see him, but I know he's there. The ground beneath my feet vibrates with his approaching steps. His shadow blocks out the sun as he looms over myself and the prick cop who still has his arms wrapped firmly around my waist. A low growl reverberates from him through me, and I can hear his barely contained rage with each ragged breath he takes.

Samuel.

"I said get your fucking hands off of her. Now." The eerie calm of his voice is more terrifying than anything.

"She attacked an officer," the cop lies, realizing at this moment exactly how badly he just fucked up. "I need to arrest her. I was going to take her around back so that she doesn't cause more of a scene than she already has."

"Attacked an officer?" Samuel repeats, questioning the man as if he didn't quite hear him right the first time.

"Yes," the cop says, his tone suggesting he is more than a

little annoyed that his authority in the situation is being called into question.

"What is your name?"

"O'Doyle."

"Well, Officer O'Doyle," Samuel says, his voice dripping with condescension, "this woman is with me."

"But-" O'Doyle starts, but is quickly cut off.

"But nothing." Samuel takes another step closer, his shadow engulfing myself and O'Doyle like storm clouds rolling in and blocking out the daylight. "I said she is with me."

"So?" O'Doyle speaks the words with a false confidence. I can feel the tremble in his body. I can't help but smirk knowing he is fucking terrified.

"So?" Samuel repeats, even calmer than before as he takes another step closer. He leans down over the two of us, but still behind me enough that I can't see his face. "So, take your goddamn hands off of her right now. Or else I will rip them from your body and hand deliver them to your children, along with the rest of your fucking corpse."

The smallest of gasps escapes O'Doyles lips before his grip around my waist starts to loosen. I push free from him, stumbling backwards a few steps. I'm careful not to break eye contact, though. Samuel places a hand gently on my elbow to help steady me before I have the chance to fall over.

I break my eye contact with Dipshit O'Doyle to look down at Samuel's hand on my elbow. He's not quite gripping my arm, but more guiding me. As if he is trying to push me behind him. My eyes trail up the length of his arm, making note of the fine lines of his tattoos peeking out from the cuff of his obviously expensive white button up shirt. His biceps are visibly hard, primed for a fight, should this altercation make such a turn. He rolls his shoulders as he pulls himself back to his full height, dwarfing both myself and O'Doyle with his massive size. I know I'm short, but Samuel is a giant by anyone's standards.

When my eyes finally find their way to Samuel's face, I am hit with a wave of some unknown emotion. The impact causes me to stumble once again. His eyes are still pinning Dipshit O'Doyle in place like the scolded dog he is. Even in profile, though, he is still one of the sexiest men I have ever laid eyes on.

"Go wait for me in the car."

Instantly, the feeling evaporates. The real reason I was in this situation comes rushing back to me in an instant. "Not on your fucking life." The words tumble out before I can catch them. I jerk my arm away from Samuel and turn my attention back to the people being herded up and shoved onto the bus like cattle.

"Now is not the time, nor is it the fucking place, woman." His words carry a weight with them, a command that I shouldn't ignore. His dark brown, unblinking eyes clouded with a darkness I had never seen before. Right now, however, I just don't fucking care.

"And when is the time and place, Samuel? Huh?" I explode, spinning on my heel to face him again. "I said no!" I am seething with rage, poking his chest with my finger as I let fly everything I have buried until now. I tell myself the jabs to his hard pectorals are causing him as much pain as I feel in my hand now. However,considering the way he doesn't even flinch, I know I'm lying to myself.

Samuel's eyes finally tear away from the still cowering Dipshit O'Doyle, who is now being led away by one of Samuel's men and taken God knows where to be dealt with. He rakes his eyes down the length of my body, stopping only for a second at my midriff, exposed from my shirt riding up during the altercation. I smooth my shirt back in place, my fingers grazing the bruise already starting to blossom just above my belly button. I wince slightly at the pain, gritting my teeth in an effort not to give away exactly how much it really hurts.

Samuel huffs out an exasperated breath, clearly annoyed with my lack of obedience.

"Listen, woman," he says, his voice grating with the sharp bite of his words.

"No, you listen," I snap back at him. "We had a deal. If I stayed, they stayed. And I fucking stayed. Through all the nasty looks, through the absolute disgusted way you sneer at me when I walk by, through every disrespect, I have fucking stayed." As I continue to rant, Samuel walks backward, causing me to step forward with him. "Now, hold up your end and get these cops out of here!"

Before I can even process what is happening, Samuel's hand is wrapped firmly around my throat. He all but lifts me in the air, turning me around, and pushing me against the side of his waiting black car. It's only now that I realize he wasn't allowing me to walk him backwards away from the crowd, but rather leading to where he wanted me to be. And now he had me right where I needed to be. Underneath his hands and powerless.

Instinctively, I reach up and start clawing at the hand around my throat. Samuel growls, taking both of my wrists effortlessly into his one free hand, and pinning them above my head. He squeezes my throat just enough to remind me exactly who is in control here. Then, he does something I never expected.

Samuel's mouth crashes against mine. I am so shocked by the feel of his lips against mine, I don't react for what feels like an eternity. When I feel his tongue pushing past my lips, I finally remember myself and clamp my teeth together to deny him entry. He doesn't relent, though. His cruel mouth continues to press into mine, bruising my lips as he tries to fight his way in. There is no way in Hell, though, that I am letting him win this war of the wills.

He pulls back for a brief moment, both of us panting from the exertion of the battle. He glared down at me, our faces still so close that our noses touched, and I glared right back at him.

There was something in his eyes, though. Something I couldn't place. Something hiding behind his rage. His dark eyes held a secret. And for the briefest of moments, I almost caught a glimpse of the man that lurked behind the facade he showed the rest of the world.

That moment passed as quickly as it had come on, though, as he stole the opportunity to reclaim my mouth while I was lost in the secrets behind his eyes. This time, I wasn't able to stop his invading tongue before he thrust it into my mouth. I push against him with my body, but he leans into me, pinning me completely against the car now. I feel every hard inch of him; his hard chest still heaving to catch his breath, the ridges of his abs, and his massive cock lengthening against my thigh. The feel of his growing erection does something to me. My knees feel weak, and the only thing keeping me upright at this time is the weight of his body against mine. Going against every instinct I have to fight, I feel myself giving in to his kiss. And I hate myself even more for it.

Samuel's lips start to slow from and become more gentle. His tongue retreats as he moves to trace my jawline with his mouth. A soft moan escapes my lips when he rakes his teeth across my neck just below my ear. "I can't decide if I want to rip your soul from that perfect little body," he whispers in my ear so that only I can hear him, "or fuck it out of you."

Samuel pulls back just enough to look down at me once again. The muscles in my jaw twitched as I ground my teeth to the point of pain. I can feel the anger burning in the pit of my stomach as he releases me from his grip, reaches over, and yanks the car door open. "Now," he growls, his rage simmering just under the arrogance of his tone, "get in the fucking car, Seraphine."

"Go to Hell." Stomping off in the direction of another officer, I ignore the feeling of Samuel's eyes burning holes in the back of my head. He doesn't stop me, though. Doesn't call out for me to get in the car. Doesn't chase after me.

Hot tears prick the backs of my eyes, threatening to fall at any second. The sound of the car door slamming behind me a few seconds later. Part of me feels a little relieved, expecting to feel the earth start to shake with Samuel's heavy footsteps as he closed the gap between us. My shoulders sag a moment later, though, when I hear the car's engine roar to life and drive away.

I scan the sea of confused faces of everyone who I had helped set up here over the last few days. Every one of them looks at me, expecting some kind of answer as to what was going to happen to them now. Some of them look away after a few seconds, accepting their fate and getting on the buses without waiting for the answer I didn't even have to give.

There was nothing I could tell them now. No words would make up for this. I had promised them a safe place to stay until I could figure out something more permanent. But I failed them. I failed them all. And as much as I wanted to blame Samuel for all of this, I knew deep down there was no one to blame but myself.

I should be headed to Eden right now. God knows I could use the money. Especially when I went to drop off the rent money I owed to the old hag I rented my apartment from and she informed me I was still short. By a lot. Apparently, she had sent out a notice a couple months raising the rent. Since I was already behind and avoiding her, I had no idea. So now, after I paid my other bills, bought a few groceries for myself, and bought some things for the others at the lot, I was broke again and didn't have enough to cover the difference.

This isn't the first time she's raised my rent since I moved in a few months ago. In fact, it's the third. Ever since she found out I started working at a strip club, she's gotten even more self righteous than she already was. This time, her excuse was I needed to pay for my lustful sins while on Earth as well as when I inevitably burn in Hell. In reality, however, it has more to do with her presumption of how much I make taking my clothes off for horny businessmen four nights a week. I doubt she would give a single fuck that I was spending the majority of the money I made on food and toiletries for the homeless.

Bills or no bills, though, there was absolutely no way I was going to the club tonight. I still had enough cash left to go out and drink this horrible day away. I couldn't stand to face that bastard right now. No doubt, I would slap the shit out of him the second I laid eyes on him. Or worse, kiss him again. *That* absolutely could never happen again.

After he left, I stood there as they continued to load everyone onto the buses and take them who knows where. I asked a few of the other cops, but no one would tell me anything. All they kept saying was I needed to speak to Samuel about it. No way that was going to happen. He lied to me about letting them stay. I had no reason to think he wouldn't lie about where he was sending them too.

That's what I get for trusting him to stay true to his word, I guess. These people have nowhere else to go, and he just shipped them off like they were unwanted packages he wanted returned to the warehouse. It took me months to find that lot, and at least another month to clean up all the used needles and broken malt liquor bottles so everyone who was displaced could set up shelter safely. Then *he* comes along and fucks it all up in less than a week.

I cross my arms over my chest, the anger boiling in my veins all over again. I catch the eye of the cabby in the rearview mirror as he drives. The look on my face is thankfully enough to warn him that it's probably better not to ask. He turns attention back to the road without a word while I continue to seeth in the backseat.

Men like Samuel don't care about people like the ones

on the lot. He's never had to worry about where his next meal would be coming from or when. He's never had to sleep under that tattered awning of a storefront just to stay out of the rain for a little while. He's never had to worry about rats or bugs getting into his bed in the middle of the night. He's never had to do any of the things I have had to do in order to survive.

I slide a twenty between the plexiglass divider and tell the driver to keep the change in the most pleasant tone I can muster as he pulls alongside the curb. Stepping out of the cab, I push the dark memories of my time on the streets away. I try my best not to dwell on that time in my life. Not like I can change anything about it now. What happened happened, and I prefer to leave it in the past where it belongs.

Exodus has always been one of my favorite nightclubs to go when I want to blow off some steam. I haven't been here in a while, though, for obvious reasons. As I pay my cover and walk past the bouncer, however, I can tell not much has really changed since I was here last.

The music hits me as soon as I walk through the blacked out door, vibrating my entire body with the sheer volume. I bypass the bar for the time being. This place is packed, even this early in the evening. I make my way through the sea of people to the edge of the crowded dance floor. I watch everyone for a moment, taking in the sight of all the different bodies grinding on each other to the beat of the thumping music. As the energy of this place starts to wash over me, I can feel the events of the day start to fade from my mind.

Closing my eyes, I let the music start to take over. I slide my hands up the sides of my body, my hips start moving to the rhythm on their own accord. As I am dancing with myself, I feel an arm snaking its way around my waist from behind, pulling me close to a hard chest and an even harder cock. Going home with someone wasn't something I was planning on doing tonight, but after what happened with Samuel, it may be just what I need.

Looking over my shoulder at the sexy stranger behind me, I lock eyes with him. I give him my best bedroom eyes as my lips twist upwards in a mischievous smile. My teeth sink into my lower lip and a soft, inaudible moan escapes me as this sexy stranger starts to grind his erection against my ass. For a second, I think about how his doesn't feel nearly as long, nor as thick as Samuel's did earlier today. I push the thought from my head, moving my hips hypnotically along with the music.

I feel his fingers tracing the waistband of my short black skirt. Leaning my head back against his shoulder, we continue to move together as I reach up and wrap my arm around his neck. My eyes roll in the back of my head when I feel his lips start to trail feather light kisses up the side of my throat. My fingers tangle in his wavy blond hair, willing him to keep going.

His fingers still tracing the space between my skirt and top slide across the exposed skin of my stomach to my hip. It doesn't quite tickle, but I feel something akin to butterflies fluttering inside me. When his hand starts going lower, I realize it's warning bells, not butterflies.

His hand slips lower and lower until it reaches the bottom hem of my skirt. He doesn't stop there, however.

Without so much as a pause, he starts inching my skirt up. Considering how short my skirt is to begin with, I know if he keeps going, I'll be flashing my pussy for everyone to see. Even as someone who takes her clothes off for money, I have my limits as to what I am willing to show. And for someone who hasn't paid for anything, that limit is zero right now.

I chuckle nervously, lowering my arm from around his neck and covering his hand with mine in an effort to stop the upward of my skirt. I try to lessen the sting of my rejection by redirecting his hand back to my hips, chalking his forwardness up to a miscommunication. I try to maintain my rhythm, hoping we can continue our dance and I can get out of here after. Preferably unscathed. I am starting to think coming out tonight wasn't the best idea.

The stranger, however, has other plans. He growls his protest at being stopped in my ear. It's so loud that I can hear it clearly even over the thumping base of the sound system. Before I can try to get away, he sinks his teeth into my shoulder. Hard. I feel a trickle of blood running down my back. I know if I try to move now, he will rip a chunk out of my skin.

Blinded by the pain of his bite, I don't have a chance to react when he locks one arm around my waist, pinning my back to his front. He shoves his other hand down the front of my top, snapping the thin spaghetti strap on one side. I rarely wear a bra, which means my breast is now fully exposed. The stranger takes the opportunity to grip my now free tit, squeezing it like a vice.

"No!" I scream in pain. The music, however, is too

loud. Despite being surrounded by so many people, no one can hear my protest.

I claw at his hands with mine, eventually prying them off of me and spinning out of his grip while desperately trying to cover myself with the remnants of my ripped shirt. He lurches forward towards me. The unmistakable haze of intoxication clouds his sapphire blue eyes. I shove hard against his chest as he reaches for me again, trying to create as much distance between us as possible so I can make my escape. He stumbles backward a step, but isn't thrown completely off balance.

Rolling my eyes, I flip my middle finger in his face and turn away from him. I don't realize my mistake until it's too late. He grabs my wrist, yanking me backwards so hard I am almost certain my shoulder dislocates from its socket. Pain shoots through my shoulder and I stumble in my platform wedge heels. He spins me around and shoves me backward until my back hits the cool bricks of the wall. My head bounces off the bricks, my vision instantly blurring with the impact. Then, he slams his hands on either side of my head as he pins me against the wall with his body, caging me in with no room to fight back. It doesn't stop me from trying, though. My efforts are useless. With his weight against me, it's impossible for me to move with enough force to escape him.

This area of the club is dark. Even though I can hear people around us, there is almost no way anyone can see us well enough to know what is going on. No doubt, even if someone were to notice us, they would just assume we were another drunken couple hooking up in the dark.

"Get the fuck off me, asshole!" I scream, still struggling

against him. I might be fighting a losing battle, but I am not about to give him the satisfaction of giving up

His laugh is lost in the sea of music and other voices around us. But I can see it in his eyes. He knows he's won. He knows I can't escape. His lips twist in a sinister smile, revealing a mouth full of yellow and brown rotting teeth. Meth teeth. No wonder he was able to break my skin with his bite so easily.

He leans in closer, his breath reeking of battery acid and whiskey. "Don't you remember me, baby?" he hisses in my ear.

"Why the fuck would I remember you?" I spit at him, wracking my fuzzy brain to try to recall the stranger's face from my memory.

"Com'on, Seraphine," he says, his voice muted by the sound of my heartbeat thundering in my ears. "I know you remember this." He forces his thigh between my legs, rubbing it against my pussy as if the movement will somehow remind me of who he is.

Fuck.

I may not remember his face, but I do remember the things I would do when I needed a fix. Things I would rather forget. Things I have worked hard to put in my past. It would seem, however, that my past keeps finding new ways of making me remember.

"I don't do that anymore," I explain, my words trembling as much as my body is now.

"Good," he snarls, his fingers digging into my thighs as he lifts the hem of my skirt. "Now I won't have to pay for a taste of this juicy cunt."

I shove against him as hard as I can one last time. The

only part of him that moves is his hand as he shoves my panties to the side. There's no use fighting anymore. The drugs are making him unnaturally stronger than his wiry build would suggest he is. I am going to need whatever strength I have left for when this is over.

Numbness washes over me as I finally accept what is about to happen. My arms fall to my sides. I turn my face away from his, hoping at least for the mercy of him finishing quickly. I swallow the bile rising in my throat when I feel the tip of his tiny cock bump against my entrance.

The colored lights dance across the wall, just inches away from my face. I focus on the neon blue and pink, blocking out everything else around me. If only those lights were a little closer, maybe someone would see what is going on and stop it from happening.But I learned a long time ago, no one was ever coming to save me.

Suddenly, just as his pathetic excuse of a dick is about to push inside me, the stranger disappears completely. I don't mean he backs away. No. He is *gone*.

My exposed body shivers at the shock of cool air as it hits my skin. My neck snaps forward so quickly, I am shocked it doesn't break. Blinking to adjust to the dim light, my eyes struggle to make out the silhouette in front of me. A red light from the dance floor shines cuts through the darkness, giving the figure an eerily evil glowing outline. I gasp as I realize the figure is holding the stranger by his throat at least a foot off the ground.

The mysterious figure ellipses me in their shadow. I am not sure they even realize I am here yet. The only details I can discern about them is how their broad chest heaves as they dangle my would-be attacker in the air. The stranger claws at the hand around his throat, gasping for a breath that doesn't come. I continue to strain my eyes against the darkness, struggling to identify my savior. If saving me is what he intends to do. It's completely possible this new stranger is simply removing his competition.

My attacker opens his mouth, but only a gurgling choking sound comes out. I let out a horrified gasp at the scene playing out before me. The figure turns towards me for the first time since he manifested out of thin air. With the light still behind him, I can't make out a single detail of his face. My attacker makes another failed attempt at speaking, choking out a single, broken sentence.

"She's. Whore. Take. Together." He sputtered out each word with what little air must be remaining in his lungs, offering to share me with this new stranger in an effort to win him over.

The figure's eyes flashed bright red. No. Not flashed. *Glowed*. If I wasn't witnessing it with my own two eyes, I would never believe it. The figure's eyes burned bright red like fires from the very depths of Hell. A familiar rage danced in their flames as he squeezed the man's throat tighter, never taking his eyes off of mine.

My entire body recoils when my savior releases a deafening roar that the music can't fully hide. A few people around us turn to see what's going on, but then shrug and return to their own drinks and dancing. The figure gives one last hard squeeze. I hear the bones in my attacker's neck crack before his entire body goes limp. The figure hardly acknowledges what he has just done, tossing the broken body deeper into the darkness for someone else to discover later when the house lights come up.

Something is wrong with me. Something is very wrong with me. I should be running. I should be outside screaming for someone to help me. I shouldn't be here, frozen in this spot with a man who just murdered someone in front of me. Most of all, I should be terrified. My body is still shaking, but not from fear. I don't know why, but I feel safer now, here, in the dark with a mysterious killer, than I ever have anywhere else.

His shoulders move up and down with each heavy breath. His shadow still looms over me, engulfing me as a reminder of how small I am compared to him. Even if I wanted to run, I know I won't make it two steps before he picks me up and drags me off who knows where to finish what pencil dick started.

My body stands frozen in place, the figures glowing eyes keeping me pinned against the wall with some unseen power. The lights from the dance floor behind him continue to keep his face hidden from me in the shadows. The entire encounter, from the moment I walked in until now, has only taken about ten minutes. It feels so much longer than that, though. Time feels like it has stopped around me. My vision blurs, and it takes a moment to realize it's because I'm crying.

The shadowy figure closes the gap between us in a single step. I pinch my eyes shut, bracing for whatever is about to happen to me. A low rumble vibrates through the figure's chest as he presses his body against mine. I don't even try to fight him off. He is at least a foot and a half taller than I am, and outweighs me by at least a hundred and fifty pounds. My previous attacker might have been slightly bigger than I am, but not like this. Not so much bigger that I didn't at least hope I could get away. As this shadow man presses his body against mine, burying his nose in my hair and inhaling deeply, grinding his massive cock against my soft belly, I know there is no escape from him.

"What do you want from me?" The question comes out as a sob. I'm not even sure he hears me at first. Then, I feel his thumb against my cheek.

The touch is so delicate, almost loving, as he catches a tear rolling down my face. He gently swipes the tear away, replacing it with a soft kiss. "I have no fucking clue."

My eyes fly open at the sound of Samuel's voice in my ear. My mouth fell open, though no words seemed to find their way out. Of all the people in all the world, why did it have to be him?

His face was still nestled in my hair, his lips brushing against the shell of my ear with each ragged breath he drew. The fight with my attacker was over, but he still sounded as if he was locked in the heat of a fierce battle.

His hand cupped the side of my face as he leaned back just enough for me to finally see his face. It was still too dark to make out all of the details, but his bright glowing eyes gave just enough light for me to be able to tell it was unmistakably Samuel. He rubs the tip of his nose down the bridge of mine, our lips touching briefly, but he didn't quite kiss me. Almost as if he didn't want to.

"I want nothing, and everything to do with you, Seraphine." My eyes flutter closed as he speaks, his thick thigh forcing my legs open wider. He has to bend his knee slightly in order to fit, pressing his leg up into my pussy until I am basically riding it. "I want you to beg for mercy." His free hand grips my hip, pulling and pushing me against him in a torturously slow rhythm. "And I want to erase every ounce of pain you have ever felt." My eyes flutter closed. The hand on my cheek slides down the side of my face, his fingers wrapping gently around the base of my throat. "I want you to kiss my feet," he says, his lips brushing against mine and his grip tightening around my neck, " while I burn this fucking world to the ground for you."

My back arches on its own accord at his words. No one has ever said anything as beautiful as this to me. It's the most erotic thing I have ever heard. I continue to rub my aching clit up and down the length of his broad thigh. My head tips back, shivers running down my spine at the sensation. My breath starts coming in heavy pants as I feel myself getting closer to the edge of climax.

Samuel's grip around my neck tightens, then quickly loosens again. He doesn't fully release me, though. I am soaking wet. No doubt, I have made a noticeable wet spot on Samuel's pants. My hips grind against his leg, desperately chasing release. With his fingers still around my throat, Samuel pulls my head forward. His lips crash against mine. I open for him immediately this time, too exhausted from everything that has happened today to fight him any longer.

Our tongues dance and tangle together, both of us trying to control the other in this moment. Samuel doesn't just kiss me. He devours my mouth, like a starving man seeing food for the first time in ages. Then, just as quickly as he began, he pulls his lips away, pressing his forehead to mine as we both struggle to regain our breath.

"That's what I want from you, Seraphine," he pants. "And it's something I will never have."

Without another word, he turns and walks away, disappearing into the sea of people, leaving me as I have always been.

Alone.

Four days. It's been four fucking days since Exodus. Four days since I broke some cocksucker's neck for touching what is mine. And I'm still so goddamn angry.

I haven't seen or heard from Seraphine since that night, either. A fact that is not helping my mood at all. I have tried calling her, but her phone is disconnected again. Something Eve has informed me happens quite often due to how much of her tips she spends taking care of those people. How can she justify going without so much to help those people? It's baffling to me. And infuriating.

I tried going by the address she had listed on her paperwork when she was hired, but that was another deadend. The address was for some homeless shelter that looked like it was closed recently. Probably the same one everyone from the lot were also residents of. From what I had gathered, though, Seraphine wasn't homeless. She had an apartment. One she couldn't really afford, I hear, but a roof over her head nonetheless.

The numbers on the screen on my laptop in front of me are nothing more than a blurry smudge at this point. I've been staring at them for at least the past hour trying to make sense of them. It's pointless, though. My brain can't focus on anything but the all-consuming rage I feel. Where in the fuck was she? And why wasn't she coming to work?

I swallow down the nagging thought that something might have happened to her after I left her, alone and half naked pressed against those cold bricks in the club. The thought of her not making it home safely is not something I am willing to entertain. I know I shouldn't have just left her there, but staying was an even more dangerous option.

It's been centuries since I have lost control like that. Scratch that. I have *never* lost control like that. Even when I rebelled, I kept my wits about me. Seeing her, though, her clothes practically ripped from her body, that lowlife's hands all over her, his pants undone. His wasn't the first life I have taken in this mortal world, but it is the first I have taken like that.

My fingers flex on the keyboard, remembering the feel of his bones breaking beneath them. Taking a life has never been something I took pleasure in doing. Taking souls is one thing. It's a business transaction, nothing more to me. A life, however, is an affront to me when there are so many other ways to make a person suffer. For instance, the asshole who tried to bribe Seraphine into more than she was willing to offer the first night I met her. I took tremendous pleasure in systematically removing his limbs, starting with the one he attempted to shove down her throat. When I was finished with him, I had Drakin burn all the pieces that remained except that one. His tiny pecker, I fed to a starving cat in the alley out back.

The only guilt I feel about ending the life of the asshole in the club is not that I killed him too quickly. I let my emotions take over, blocking out every instinct I have and snapped his neck like a toothpick. He didn't deserve a quick death. Especially after trying to bargain with me. *Me*, of all creatures!

I slam my laptop closed, ignoring the sound of the screen breaking as it lands against the keys. Leaning back in my chair, I pinch the bridge of my nose, tilt my head back, and exhale a defeated breath. *Where the fuck is she?*

A knock at my office door pulls me from my thoughts. "What?" I bark, not bothering to hide my frustration.

"Glad to see you're in a pleasant mood, as usual, Light Bringer." I sit straight up in my chair at the sound of the voice of the person entering my office right now.

Fuck. Of all the people I could have predicted to be walking through my door right now, she was definitely not one of them. "To what do I owe the pleasure, Lilith?"

"Oh, come now, Light Bringer," she laughs as she closes and locks the door behind her. Her voice has the same melodic malevolent tone I remember. "Don't sound so disheartened to see me."

Rolling my eyes, I reopen my laptop, pretending not to notice the unreadable screen. "You know better than anyone, Lilith, I was never very good at faking human emotions. If I sound disheartened, it's because I am." I start typing randomly, hoping she takes the hint. She doesn't, instead flopping down on the leather couch and making herself at home.

It's been at least half a century since I last saw Lilith. I glance over at her from the corner of my eye as she surveys my office. She has changed many times since her expulsion from The Garden. This new look definitely suits her, though. Her dark hair is cut short, just touching the tops of her shoulders, with fiery streaks of red throughout. She crossed one long leg over the other, her short skirt riding up her muscular thigh almost to her hip. She's added a few more tattoos since I last saw her as well. The black crop top she is wearing shows off the roses and thorns winding up the side of her toned abdomen. A testament to her origins, no doubt.

Humankind's first advocate for equality. The forgotten first wife of Adam. Mother of Demons. Well, not really the mother of demons. She's not the mother of anyone, actually. God cast her out for essentially the same reason Eve was cast out. She refused to play the part she was given. She disobeyed. Just as I disobeyed. The difference between her and Eve, however, is that while Eve was saddened by her curse, Lilith was enraged by hers.

Unlike Eve, she turned her back on God. She spent her long years fueling her hatred for her Creator, doing everything in her power to corrupt as many people as she could. Lilith may not be able to take a soul, like I can, but she ensured God didn't get them either.

"Can't you muster up at least a little joy at the sight of an old friend?" she asks, cocking an eyebrow in my direction. "And I haven't gone by that name in at least two decades."

"And what are the covens calling you now?" I huff, not bothering to look up from my screen.

"My men who work under me call me Havoc, now," she says, her voice laced with pride.

"The men who work under you?" I repeat, incredulously. "That's a funny way of saying 'the men I am currently fucking'."

"You know me much better than that, Light Bringer," she says, rising to her seat in a smooth, fluid motion, and sauntering over to me. "The only one I take pleasure in working under me is you." Leaning down so her perky tits are inches from my face, spinning my chair toward her. Havoc's emerald green eyes work their way down, settling on the bulge between my legs. The corners of her mouth turned upward, a silent invitation matching the lust in her eyes. "So, how about you stop pretending to work on a broken fucking laptop," she says in a deceptively calm, yet sensuous voice, softly lowering the broken screen without taking her hands off my crotch, "and fuck me right here on this expensive new desk of yours."

My skin burns, threatening to explode off my body in an instant. I can feel the heat in my eyes. My veins boil and I can feel the anger swelling in my chest. When Havoc's hands move from the arm of my chair to go for my belt, it takes every ounce of composure I have left in me not to snap.

I grab her wrists before she has a chance to touch me any more than she already has. Her eyes snap up to meet mine, a mischievous gleam hiding just behind the bright green color.

"Get out, Havoc." I make no effort to hide the disdain in my voice.

Havoc's face shifts to a playful pout. She lets out a small

whimper of disappointment before smiling. Her smile fades instantly, though, when she tries to move her hands again towards my belt and I deny her again. "Wait, what?" she says, her nose scrunching in confusion.

"Did I fucking stutter?" I bark, shoving her backwards by her wrists. She stumbles back a few steps, her jaw dropping as she regains her footing.

"What the fuck is going on with you?" she scoffs. "You've never turned this pussy down."

"Well, there's a first time for everything."

"No," she says, studying my every move as I swivel my chair away from her. "Something is different with you, Light Bringer. Something...." she hesitates for a moment, carefully selecting her next words as she crosses her arms over her impressive chest, "less than."

"Less than?" I chuckle, not even bothering to look up at her as I rifle through some inconsequential documents on my desk.

"Yes," she says, almost cautiously. "Less than...well, everything I have ever known you to be. You've lost your edge. I just can't seem to figure out why."

"In the famous words of a great Greek philosopher I met in a bar once, sucks to suck I guess." I am growing tired of this conversation. I want her gone so I can continue to accomplish nothing while I worry about the whereabouts of Seraphine in peace.

She places both hands on my desk, leaning over my desk close to my ear. "If I remember correctly, you and that Greek guy fucked the hell out of me for three days straight before you took his soul." I flick my eyes back up to hers as she pulls back.

A heavy silence hangs in the air between us. Havoc studies my face for any hint she can manipulate to her advantage. I hold her gaze, not giving her anything she can use against me.

A ping from my phone on the desk breaks the silence. My eyes slide over to see a text from Drakin on the illuminated screen.

DRAKIN

She's here.

Two words. More than enough to give Havoc exactly what she needs. The corners of her mouth twist up. Darkness moves across her face. "So that's why."

"Get. Out." I don't deny anything. I don't confirm anything, either, though. I know what she is capable of. And I will make her immortal live an actual living Hell if she touches a single golden hair on Seraphine's head. She knows this.

She smirks, giving me a final up and down. "See you around, Light Bringer," she says. Turning on her heels, she unlocks the door and walks out the door.

It clicks closed behind her. I half expected her to slam it. Then again, that's not Havoc's style. Her style is much more...terrifying than simply slamming a door and storming out.

All the hairs on the back of my neck stand at attention. The air suddenly feels charged with electricity, like lightning just before a strike. A storm is definitely on the horizon. And if Havoc is involved, it will be a storm of biblical proportions.

ELEVEN

There's a loose thread on my shirt tickling my forearm. It's driving me crazy, but I'm pretty sure if I pull it the entire shirt will fall apart. Looking up the stairs leading to the second floor of Eden, I probably shouldn't be thinking about a loose thread on a shirt I got over five years ago, but for some reason, it's all I can think about.

I take a deep breath in through my nose, blowing it slowly out through my mouth, just like my counselor taught me to do when I feel anxious. It's supposed to help calm me down so I don't feel like using other means to do so. As I repeat the process again and again, the thumping in my chest leads me to believe it might not be working as well as it has in the past.

What the fuck was I thinking coming back here? I could have just left. I *should* have just left. I didn't have enough cash, though, to move away right now. Missing the past few days of work hadn't exactly helped my financial situation, either. Plus, I wanted to know what happened to everyone when they were removed from the lot.

I had been asking around some of the other homeless communities, the ones who preferred to stay under bridges and in back allies. No one knew anything, not that I was expecting them to, anyway. These communities were mostly populated by users who were not interested in getting clean. Because of this, they weren't allowed to stay at the shelter before it was shut down. They were wary of anyone who wasn't one of them. The only reason they talked to me at all is because I was known in their circles from my previous time on the streets.

I know everyone from the lot hadn't just disappeared. After the interaction with Samuel, the cops wouldn't tell me much. Just that they were given orders by their captain to load everyone up and relocate them. No one would tell me where they would be relocated to, though. I had a feeling they had been told not to tell me where. Another manipulation by Samuel. He was making sure I would have to come to him for the information.

Another reason to add to the list why I hated him so much. He had planned this. He wanted to be the only one I could come to for help. He wanted me on my knees, begging for his help. I wasn't going to give him the satisfaction of groveling at his feet to know where he had moved everyone, though. Then, the incident at the club happened.

I still haven't fully processed what happened that night. One minute, I had resigned myself to my fate of being taken by that asshole in the club. The next minute, Samuel was there. He saved me from being violated. He killed that guy,

I'm sure of it. I heard the bones break in his neck. I saw the way his lifeless body crumpled to the ground when Samuel tossed him aside like an old ragdoll. I felt the heat on Samuel's skin when he pinned me to the wall. Still, it felt like some kind of dream. His eyes. The way they glowed. It wasn't...human.

I shook my head, chuckling to myself as I took the first few steps upward. It was crazy, the things my imagination had come up with over the past few days to explain what I saw. It was just the lights. I'm sure of it. I was terrified and my mind was playing tricks on me because of it. That was the only logical explanation. At least, that's what I had to keep telling myself.

Walking up the steps to Samuel's office on the second floor felt more like a descent into Hell. Each step up seemed to pull me further down. I had no idea what I was going to say to him. Thank you for saving me? How did you even know where I was? Where the fuck did you take my friends?

I stopped a few steps from the top, trying once again to figure out what I was going to say to him. Trying and failing to think of what to say. *If* he even wants to talk to me, that is. I mean, I wouldn't want to talk to someone whom I saved who then ghosted me for four days. Why should he?

The sound of a door closing above me, pulls me out of my own thoughts. I look up, expecting to see Drakin or one of the men who work for Samuel. My heart sinks into my stomach when I look up and see a tall, gorgeous woman turning away from the office door. She pauses when she notices me standing there, looking equally as stunned to see me as I do her. Her expression quickly changes, however, shifting from surprise to superiority in the blink of an eye.

"If you're who I think you are, he's waiting for you," she smirks as she begins her descent down the stairs.

My mouth falls open as I try to force out some kind of explanation as to who I am and how she must have confused me with someone else, but nothing comes out. I make a few stammering sounds, but nothing resembling words.

"Oh, you are *definitely* who I think you are," she laughs. Her bright green eyes glitter with venomous hatred, betraying her jovial tone.

She takes another step down towards me. Instinctively, I take a step back. She pauses when she notices this, looking me up and down as if measuring my worth and finding me lacking. She gives me another smirk. "Timid, I see. He typically doesn't go for timid."

"What do you mean?" I'm not sure if she meant it as an insult, but that's exactly how I took it.

She huffs, but doesn't answer the question. The strange woman takes another step closer, now standing on the small landing with me, and reaches out towards me. I flinch reflexively as she wraps a piece of my hair around her finger. "What is your name?"

"Why?"

"Because I want to know." She continues to play with the piece of hair, studying it closely without making eye contact with me.

I swallow hard, trying to decide if I should answer her truthfully or not. "Seraphine."

Her finger stops moving, but she doesn't drop the piece

of hair. Every muscle in my body goes rigid. My chest rises and falls with rapid breaths, but I remain as calm as possible. The air around us grows thick with an unseen tension. It feels like an eternity before she moves.

"The two of you have more in common that I realized," she whispers, more to herself than to me, as she wraps my hair tighter around her finger. I draw in a sharp breath as the tension starts to hurt my scalp.

I start looking around frantically, searching for any opportunity to get away from this woman. I'm about to take my chances and run up the stairs to hide in the private room opposite Samuel's office until I can get out of the building entirely when, suddenly, she drops my hair and continues down the stairs as if nothing happened. "See ya around, Little Flame," she says over her shoulder. "I'm sure our paths will cross again."

I watch her until she disappears through the door at the bottom of the stairs, a burst of loud music pouring in as she opens the door, then muting again as it closes behind her. I stare at the closed door for a moment, trying to process the interaction that just took place. As if I didn't have enough questions floating around in my head already, now this.

Tilting my head, my eyes focus on the top of the stair only a few feet above me. She, whoever she was, had come from Samuel's office. I swallowed down the bile rising in my throat at all the reasons why she would have been up there. In the few days since his arrival at Eden, I had only ever seen Drakin, Eve, and a handful of other men be allowed access up here. Honestly, when I arrived today asking to speak with him, I fully expected to be told no or to wait in the back. Yes, he had sent for me once to speak with him in his private room, but that was only so he could gloat about being my new boss. His office seemed to be off limits to everyone who wasn't in his inner circle. A circle I was most definitely not a part of. But she was.

Taking a deep breath, I remind myself it didn't matter who she was or why she had just come from his office. I was only here to thank him for what he did for me and to find out where he had sent my friends. This wasn't a social call. What he did and who he did it with was no concern of mine. So, why did I have this knot in my stomach with all the images in my head of what she might have been doing with him before I showed up?

My knees felt like jello and my legs felt like lead as I started up the stairs again. By some miracle, I didn't fall. Standing in front of the dark mahogany door, I hesitated before knocking. My emotions were all over the place. I was angry for what he had done that day on the lot, thankful for what he had done at the club that night, and aroused by the memory of his body pressed against mine as he kissed me. The emptiness I have felt every day since he left me alone in the darkness.

This would be the last time I saw him. I am certain I no longer have a job after not showing up this week. I stiffened my spine and knocked twice on the door. Yes, this would be the last time I would have to deal with this entitled goddamn asshole. I would get the information I needed, thank him for what he did for me, and leave. Like he left me.

After a moment of silence, I knocked again, thinking he must not have heard the first time. My shoulders slump when I am met with nothing but silence on the other side of the door. I know he is inside. One of the security guys told me when I arrived he'd been up here for hours, and that woman on the stairs a moment ago all but said he was still there. There is only one other explanation as to why I am getting no answer when I knock. He's ignoring me.

This realization infuriates me. After everything, after he basically kidnapped my friends, after he abandoned me half naked and soaking fucking wet from that goddamn kiss, *he* is ignoring *me*? I don't fucking think so.

I open the door without waiting for an invitation. The room is dimly lit. The only light is a red glow coming through the one-way glass overlooking the main stage area just below the office window. Even the harsh fluorescent light from the hallway struggles to permeate the darkness. My eyes take a moment before they adjust and settle on the silhouette of Samuel standing in front of the window, looking out over his domain.

The dim redness clings to the outline of his body like an evil halo as he stands with his back to me. The curves of his hard muscles seem to soften in the glow that envelopes him, but doesn't consume him. It's almost like the darkness I feel when I look at him, the darkness I feel inside him when he is near, is fighting to keep the light around him at bay.

Samuel doesn't acknowledge my presence in the room. For a moment, I convince myself he truly doesn't know I am here. Slamming the door closed behind me, his resigned, annoyed sigh tells me otherwise. Even when I am standing less than ten feet away from him, he is still ignoring me in the hopes I will go away.

"Was I not clear enough before, Havoc?" His words are clipped and cold. More so than usual. Hatred radiates off of him like unseen flames. "Go. The fuck. Away." He enunciates each word clearly and with such malice, but he never turns around.

I study his outline in silence. He is so tall. I remember how his shadow eclipsed me in the club as he stood over me. The way his neck craned down to kiss me. The way I had to push myself up on my toes to kiss him back.

Even in the darkness, I can see the thickness of his tight muscles straining against the black dress shirt he wears. His back is firmly sculpted, narrowing only slightly at his waist. His arms quiver with need for a violent release as he slides his hands in his pockets. Even his thighs seemed poised for a fight. I can't see his face, but I am certain his full lips are pursed in a hard line, the way I have seen them do when he is trying to keep his composure.

My betraying body remembers the way those lips felt on mine. My own lips tingle at the memory. A pulse starts to beat in my aching pussy. My skin heats and I feel my nipples harden beneath the thin fabric of the sundress I stupidly decided to wear today.

No, I tell myself. I will not lose focus. I am here for answers. Answers he purposefully has kept from me so I would have to come to him. I will ask him where he sent my friends and thank him for saving me the other night. That's all. I won't let him scramble my senses again with his mouth in any way; words or otherwise.

"I'm not Havoc," I snort with derision, crossing my arms over my chest.

His head whips around in shock at the sound of my voice. "Seraphine." His demeanor changes in an instant. Every muscle seems to relax at once, as if they had not been able to do so in a long time. His relief only lasts a few seconds, however, as his brows knit together in anger again. "Where in the unholy *fuck* have you been?"

My nails dig into my palms as he stalks towards me, closing the distances between us in three heavy steps. I open my mouth to answer, but he cuts me off with a bruising kiss that steals all the air from my lungs.

I punch and shove at his chest with everything I have, but he doesn't budge. Instead, he grabs both of my wrists in one of his hands, pinning them above my head. I buck my hips, trying to get my legs high enough to kick him off of me, but he is too close. He presses the full weight of his body against me, rendering me immobile and at his mercy.

Mercy. Ha! Samuel shows no mercy as he plunders my mouth with his tongue. I struggle and fight against him, but it's useless. There's no denying him what he wants. There's no denying what I want. And, right now, we both want the same thing.

Suddenly, as quickly as he started, Samuel stops and takes a step back, dropping my wrists. They fall, feeling like lead at my sides. Both of us heave in heavy gulps of much needed air. His eyes go dark, but I swear I see the red glow simmering behind the blackness. His gaze rakes down the length of my body before slowly traveling back to meet mine. The need to close the distance between us is almost unbearable. Every ounce of my being wants to feel him. I take a step towards him, only for him to take a step back in unison.

If he would have slapped me, it wouldn't have hurt as badly as this silent rejection does now. He lowers his eyes in shame, turning away and walking back over to the window.

"Leave. Now." Two words spoken barely above a whisper, and I feel something inside me begin to break. Three times now, he has kissed me. Three times I have kissed him back. When I finally give in, he kicks me out? What the fuck?

"No." The word slices through the tension in the room like a knife. "I need to know where they are, Samuel."

His shoulders move up and down with the ragged breath he draws in. "They are safe. That's all you need to know."

"That's not all I need to know, goddammit!" Hurt and anger mix inside me. I feel the hot tears forming in my eyes.

Without a word, Samuel slams his fist against the glass of the window. It cracks into a spider web around his hand. "I said leave." His words are calm, which makes them all the more terrifying.

"I'm not leaving until I know where they are," I say through clenched teeth.

"For once, woman," he growls, angling his head slightly towards me so that I see the hardness of his jaw, "will you do as you are fucking told."

"No."

He lands another punch against the cracked glass. "It's not safe for you right now." I don't respond, confused and silently willing him to elaborate further. "*You* are not safe right now."

"Why am I not safe, Samuel?" I ask in whispered confusion.

"I am not safe for you. Here. Now." He pauses, the veins in his neck straining as he swallows hard. "Please, leave, Seraphine. I don't want to hurt you."

I stand, frozen in place at the pain in his voice. He is

holding back. For me. Because he doesn't want to hurt me. What he has failed to realize, however, is that there is nothing he can do to hurt me that others haven't forced on me in the past. I am stronger than he gives me credit for. And I am not walking away this time.

"The only thing hurting me right now," I say, dropping my voice to a low and seductive tone, "is not having you inside me right now."

His fist resting against the glass flexes, making a crunching sound as tiny droplets of blood drip from his knuckles. "Don't do this," he pleads. "I am barely able to contain myself as it is."

Reaching behind me, I click the lock on the office door into place, sealing my own fate. I slide my fingers up my arm, pushing one thin strap of my dress down. "You told me once, you couldn't decide if you wanted to rip my soul from my body," I purr, repeating the motion on the other side, "or fuck it out of me." Samuel looks over his shoulder. "If it's all the same to you," I tell him as my dress slips from my naked body into a crumpled pool of fabric at my feet, "I'll take the latter."

TWELVE

SAMUEL

Fucking. Unholy. Hell.

I knew Seraphine was gorgeous, but nothing could have prepared me for the sight of her naked and offering herself to me. My sacrificial lamb, ready to be eaten alive.

Her skin looked like she bathed in milk every night. Her silvery blonde hair glittered in the light shining in from the window. Every curve of her body looked as if it had been carved by the most skilled of artists from the rarest marble in the world. The angels of Heaven didn't hold a candle to the beauty Seraphine possessed.

She looked even more delicate in the dim, red light that bathed the room. Her pale skin seemed almost luminescent. Her perfect tits begged to be bitten. There was a small patch of white-blonde hair neatly trimmed sitting just above the glistening slit of her pussy. Her toned dancer legs were longer than one would expect for someone of her height. Her seductive young body was like nothing I had ever seen. Gentle and ethereal; her overwhelming beauty a sharp contrast to the ugliness I am used to. The innocence of her appearance makes me want her even more than I already do.

I am not good. No one in the span of eternity, even before my fall from grace, has ever accused me of being so. I want nothing more than to break this woman, shattering her very being into a thousand pieces before reconstructing her into the goddess I know she is. I want to dominate her in ways she has never known could possibly exist, no matter how it will ruin her for any other man in the process. No, I am not good, and I know this. The one time I try to be good, to do the right thing and let her walk away before I turn her world upside down with a snap of my fingers, the universe won't let me.

Still, I tried to hold back. I gave her one last chance to leave. One last chance to save herself from the pain. One last chance to walk away, live the rest of her life, and not to ruin her forever with the Hell that consumes me. Seraphine has made her choice. No one, not even God, can help her now.

Thank fuck for that.

The moment I heard the lock click into place, I knew there was no way I would be able to hold myself back anymore. I have never taken anyone by force, and I had no intentions of starting tonight. But hearing that lock told me she was done fighting this as much as I was.

I close the distance between us without a word. The time for talking has passed. In one smooth motion, I hook my hands under the curve of her ass, lifting her off her feet. She instinctively wraps her legs around my waist as I slam her back against the wall. The diamond hard peaks of her nipples press against my chest through my shirt.

"Last chance, woman," I growl through gritted teeth,

grinding my hard bulge against her warm pussy. "There is no going back after this."

"What the fuck makes you think I would want to go back?" she hisses, sinking her teeth into the flesh of her bottom lip as her hips start to rock against me. Her head falls back and her eyes flutter closed. A soft moan escapes her lips as she presses herself against me. My cock slides effortlessly between her puffy pussy lips, already soaked with her own juices.

My answering laugh is evil even to my own ears. I shift her weight so I am holding her with one hand, all but ripping the zipper of my trousers down to free my cock. "You're fucking mine now, woman."

My lips cover hers at the same moment I shove my cock inside her soaking wet cunt, burying myself to the hilt. I swallow her scream as she takes every inch of me inside her. Her nails dig into my shoulders through my shirt I have yet to remove. The pain mixes with the softness of the material.

Humility has never been one of my strengths. I know exactly how I measure up against mortal men. Which is to say, I don't. I surpass them in every way possible, and I know it. The fact that she takes my length with such ease is impressive. Despite not being a virgin, I know she will bleed when we are finished from the sheer size of me, alone.

I hold myself inside her, not moving for a long moment, giving us both time to adjust to the sensations. Godfuckingdammit, she is so fucking tight. So tight, I am afraid I might bust before either of us wants me to. I've had hundreds upon hundreds of pussies in my many lifetimes, but hers is by far the best I have ever felt. I know she will forever be ruined now for anyone else, but I am just as certain that I am equally ruined, as well.

She pulls away just enough to look down at the connection between us, her mouth agape as she gasps for air. I follow her gaze downward, still holding her hips firmly against mine. The fingers of my free hand trace the line of her collarbone, the milky color of her skin flushes under my touch as the tips of my fingers continue their journey. Her throat is so warm as I wrap my hand around it. Her breath quickens and a mischievous smile spreads slowly across her angelic face as I squeeze just enough for her to feel the control I now hold over her.

"Move," she commands between gasps.

The corners of my lips twist upward in a sinister smile. Watching her expression as I move, I pull my hips slowly backwards. She takes a sharp inhale at the feel of my thick cock sliding inside her. I almost leave her completely, stopping before my tip has a chance to escape this new found heaven. When I slam my hips forward, her entire body jolts upwards against the wall. She buries her head into my shoulder, screaming again in ecstasy.

"Again," she whimpers, desperate need filling her voice.

"Such a demanding little cunt," I chuckle as I repeat the backwards motion with my hips. "What makes you think you get to tell me how to fuck you?"

Seraphine doesn't get the opportunity to answer, though, before I slam myself forward again. This time, however, I don't stop. With each thrust, I stake my claim on her body, her breath, her mind, and her fucking soul. No part of her will be left untouched by me. "Take it, woman," I grit out. "Take this cock like I know you can." Her only response is a determined growl followed by an intangible garble of what I can only assume were words.

With her entire body pinned against the wall, she moves as best she can in a desperate attempt to match my thrusts as I relentlessly pound her cunt. Her jaw clenches in obvious frustration as she tries to reposition herself. Chuckling at her futile attempt to move me, to gain any kind of control, I spin us both around without warning.

Holding her tight against me so we never break contact, I lower myself onto the leather couch. "On your fucking knees, woman," I command, pushing her down to the floor.

Seraphine hisses as my cock slips from inside her, but she doesn't dare protest. She drops to her knees obediently. Without another word, she wraps her slender fingers around my dick as best she can with one hand. There is at least half an inch between the tip of her thumb and forefinger, like I assumed there would be. Leaning forward, she spits on the tip of my cock. Moving her hand up and down, she strokes me from base to tip, lubing up my cock before taking me into her mouth.

And what a fucking mouth it is.

My head falls back onto the couch as her tongue curls around the underside of my dick. She pushes herself down as far as her throat will allow her to go. As she works her way upward, she gives that extra sensitive spot at the base of my head a teasing flick with the tip of her tongue. It takes every ounce of strength I possess not to blow my load down the back of her throat instantly. Her eyes flick up to mine, flickering with a wickedness that tells me she knows exactly what she is doing to me.

With her hands still around my cock, I tangle my fingers

in her hair with one hand, angling her face upward to me. I lean forward as I grab her by the throat once again, this time pulling her so that her face is a mere inches from mine. She laughs maniacally, reveling in her ability to momentarily gain a semblance of control over me.

"If you make me cum before I am ready," I growl, "I will edge you until you are nothing more than a quivering mess at my feet. Do you understand me?" Seraphine nods as best she can with my hand around her neck. I tug her hair and apply slightly more pressure to the sides of her throat. "Use your fucking words."

"Y-yes, Samuel," she manages to force out, excitement dancing in the stormy gray of her eyes.

"That's my good little slut." I release her throat, but not her hair, holding her head in place. A loud crack fills the room and her head snaps to the side as my now free hand connects with her cheek in a hard slap. A bright red handprint blossoms on the side of her face. Her deviant smile widens as she turns and tilts her head back up to me.

She laughs dementedly as I fist her hair with both hands now. Her mouth opens wide and she sticks out her tongue, begging for more without a word. I spit into her mouth before shoving her face down onto my cock, more than happy to oblige her in this silent request.

Holding her head still by her hair, I fuck her face mercilessly. Seraphine gags and coughs, saliva dripping from her chin and her eyes welling up with tears from the relentless assault on her mouth. She can't take the full length of me, but that doesn't stop either of us from trying.

Inch by inch, she sucks more of me into that glorious mouth of hers. I can feel her swallow down the drops of precum leaking from my tip. Each satisfied moan she makes vibrates up my shaft, making my balls tingle.

When the head of my dick finally touches the back of her throat, I hold her in place, reveling in the sounds she makes as she chokes. When I feel her fingers tap against the side of my thigh, I release her hair immediately, allowing her to take the breath she desperately needs.

Seraphine falls backwards, her knees sliding out from under her as she collapses to the floor. She gasps and chokes as she drags each gulp of air into her lungs. I give her a brief reprieve before leaning forward and grabbing her delicate wrist, pulling her into my lap. I am not a monster, but I am, after all, the Devil. And I want more.

"Ride my cock." I dig my fingers into the meat of her ass, jackhammering myself into her. Placing her hands on my shoulders, she raises and lowers herself in perfect unison with me. Over and over again, she takes it all. I can feel the wetness leaking out of her, soaking through the pants I have still not fully removed. Her pussy grips my thick cock like a vice, squeezing me in the most torturously delicious way possible. I slide my hand across her taut stomach, noticing the way it concaves more than it probably should, and pushing my thumb between her lips until I find her clit.

"Oh!" she moans. "Dear, God, yes."

A growl rumbles through my chest. "I am not God, Seraphine," I bark, circling her swollen clit with my thumb as I hammer into her from below even harder. "You will have no other before me. No one after me. Ever." The mention of that name fuels something inside me. Something sinister and dark. I wanted to erase that name from her tongue. I want to burn my own name in its place so that it is the only one she knows. "No man. No woman. No fucking God." Her mouth falls open and I can feel her walls starting to spasm around me. She is so close. I pull her to my chest as she continues to ride me. "I am the Devil, Seraphine," I rasp in her ear. "From this moment on, I fucking possess you." Pressing down on her clit, I slam myself into her one last time.

Thank fuck this room is soundproof. I roar until my voice cracks as I pour myself into her before clamping my teeth down on her shoulder. Seraphine's resulting scream is followed by a flood as she cums around me. We both explode into a million pieces. My vision blurs momentarily, and I feel my skin beginning to rip apart at the seams. I take a few steadying breaths, bringing myself back under control before things take a turn neither of us is ready for.

Seraphine collapses against my chest, her eyes still closed as she comes down from the high of her orgasm. The world around me begins to clear as my dick twitches inside her. Neither of us speaks as our chests heave against one another. I feel her heart beating behind her ribs, the rhythm slowing from a hard thundering to a more gentle pace. The sweet smell of sex mixes with the sweat beading across both of our bodies. Even that starts to dissipate after a few moments.

The reality of what just happens slowly starts to creep into the peripheral edges of my mind. I push the nagging voice aside, not ready to deal with the consequences of my actions just yet. For what feels like an eternity, even to me, only the sound of our breathing as it returns to normal fills the room.

"Forever?" Seraphine asks out of nowhere. Her

question echoes in the heavy silence like a church bell after a funeral.

"Forever what?" I ask flatly.

"You said you would possess me," she explains. Her voice is small, almost sounding terrified, like a child asking a question which they are afraid to know the answer to. "Will you possess me forever?"

I slide my hands across the perfectly smooth skin of her back, enveloping her in my arms like a shield. Her body trembles against mine. Her heated skin begins to cool as the sweat dries against it. Pressing a chaste kiss against her silvery blonde hair, I answer the way you answer a child when they ask such things.

"Forever," I lie.

THIRTEEN

The faint sound of keys clicking on a keyboard pulls me from my dreamless sleep. I pinch my eyes tightly, fighting to stay asleep for just a little bit longer. It's completely useless, though. I've always been a light sleeper. Years of living on the streets will condition you to never fall into too deep of a sleep in order to stay vigilant of your surroundings. I'm so exhausted, however, I can barely muster the strength to open my eyes.

My limbs feel like they are filled with concrete as I stretch, trying to rouse myself awake enough to get out of bed. But this isn't my bed. This isn't a bed at all. This mattress is too firm and this blanket covering me is way too soft to be one of the thrift store covers I use.

Fuck.

I'm in Samuel's office, on Samuel's couch, under Samuel's blanket, with Samuel's cum inside me.

I slowly lifted my lashes trying to determine if I could possibly slip out of the room without him noticing. My eyes were still blurry from sleep, taking longer than I wanted for them to focus. When they do, I can see the source of the incessant clicking is Samuel typing on a laptop at his desk.

The glow from the screen illuminated his face, but not much else in the room. He seemed to be deeply concentrating on whatever it was he was working on. As I pulled myself up, making sure to hold the black fleece blanket close to my chest, he didn't even acknowledge my presence in the room with him. Perhaps he was enthralled enough in his work that I could slip out without being detected.

I stood up from the couch, careful to not lose my balance on my still gelatin-like legs, and managed to retrieve my dress from the floor where I had discarded it earlier without him looking up once. This was proving to be easier than I thought it would be. So why did it make my chest ache?

I glanced over my shoulder one last time at Samuel. The laptop looked like a child's toy compared to his size. I opened my mouth to say goodbye, but closed it again without a word. It was obvious he didn't give a shit that I was leaving. There's no way he hasn't seen me, which means he is actively trying not to. No point in telling someone goodbye when they don't want you here in the first place.

After pulling the dress over my head, I place my hand on the doorknob, turning it as slowly and quietly as possible so as to not disturb him further. I don't get even one foot out the door before I hear a deep and angry growl from behind me.

"Take one step out that door, woman, and I'll put you over my fucking knee."

I freeze midstep. Not because he has threatened me, but because I am debating if I want the promised spanking more than I want to leave. Swallowing hard, I push the images of my naked ass burning bright red by his hands as I am splayed across his lap from my mind. Once was a mistake, a means to an end. Twice would be an irresponsible choice. I've already made enough of those for one lifetime.

I take a step backwards, closing the door without turning away from it. The sound of the mechanism clicking into place as the door closes sounds like a grenade going off in the silence of the room. Even with my back to him, the weight of the tension between bears down on my chest.

"Pitty," he sighs, his fingers resuming their rhythmic clicking across his keyboard.

"Why?" I ask, my voice sounding so small it infuriates me.

"Why what?"

"Why is it a pity?"

He pauses for a moment, the sound of the keys stopping. "Because I would have enjoyed taking you over my knee more than having you stand there with your fucking back to me like a petulant child."

Spinning around on my heel, I can feel my blood boiling in my veins at his remark. "I'm a child?" I repeat, finding my voice again.

"Yes, Seraphine," he barks as he places his hands on his desk and rises from his chair. "You are acting like a child."

"How the fuck am I acting like a child? You're the one who didn't even look at me when I got up!"

"Because you were the one running away!"

"I wasn't running away, asshole! I was going home!"

"Call it whatever you like, but it is still running."

I open my mouth to scream at him some more, but he slams the palm of his hand down before I can speak. His eyes darken as we stare each other down. The now familiar red glow burns around the edges of his irises. My cheeks burn and the back of my throat still stings from our previous activities. Neither of us moves. Neither of us breathes. Neither of us say a goddamn word.

As if we were both struck by the same jolt of electricity, we jolt forward at the same time. Samuel effortlessly pushes his huge desk aside in a single, smooth motion. I sprint forward, leaping into his arms and colliding with his chest. Our mouths crash together like stars exploding in the night sky. With his hands holding me up from underneath me, he walks us over to the couch and lays me back down on the supple leather.

"Why do you test me, woman?" he breathes against my lips.

"Because I fucking can."

His only response is to stake his claim on my lips again, bruising them in a violent kiss before pulling away to stand over me. "Go back to sleep," he says, turning away to collect the blanket from where I had dropped it on the floor a moment ago. "Drakin will drive us back to my place when I am finished here."

"I really just want to go back to my apartment," I tell him, pushing myself up on my elbows.

"Nonsense," he says, returning with the blanket and placing it over me as if he is tucking a toddler in for the night.

"It's not nonsense," I say, a little offended that he would call my home nonsense. "I need to take a shower and change clothes and I can't do that at your place."

"You think I don't have a shower at my apartment?" he scowls, standing over me with his arms crossed over his chest.

"You don't have my clothes."

"I'll send out for some new clothes for you."

"You can do that?"

"Yes," he says with a confused expression.

Shaking my head, I decide to not go down that rabbit hole with him right now. Obviously, he's always had money so he doesn't understand that not everyone knows that you can order clothes the same way you order pizza, apparently. "Doesn't matter. What matters is, I am going home."

I throw the blanket aside and stand up, only for Samuel to immediately push me back down again. He leans over me, placing his hands on the back of the couch on either side of my head so I can't attempt to stand again.

"Maybe I wasn't clear enough, Seraphine," he says in a low, deceptively calm voice. "We are going to my apartment when I finish my work. It's not a question."

I close my eyes, trying to find the words to express to him why I can't go with him to his apartment. "Samuel," I start, already feeling the tears stinging behind my eyelids, "I need to go home. Please."

He doesn't say anything, but I can still feel his warm breath against my neck. A moment that feels like an hour passes before he presses a gentle kiss to the side of my throat. "I'll come with you."

"Samuel, n-" He cuts me off by sinking his teeth into my shoulder. I half moan and half scream at the sensation.

"Why do you have to be so difficult, woman?" he whispers in my ear.

"Why do you have to be such an asshole?" I giggle.

"Because I'm the Devil, Seraphine."

"I'm starting to see that."

FOURTEEN

SERAPHINE

My foot taps rapidly as Drakin makes the turn onto the street I live on. I stare out the window at all of the abandoned houses I have never really paid much attention to since I moved here. I never saw anything wrong with them until now. In my world, empty houses and overgrown lawns were normal. Now that I was driving past them in a car that cost more than any place I have ever lived, however, I couldn't help but feel a little ashamed at the neighborhood I call home.

Samuel places a hand on my shaking knee. I have felt his eyes on me most of the drive here, but I can't bring myself to look at him right now. In less than a quarter mile, he is going to see the dump I've been living in for the past few months. He's going to smell the rotten garbage from the dumpster out back that hasn't been emptied since before I moved in. He's going to see the nonexistent kitchen, the particle board bathroom walls, and the holes in them I still haven't patched up. He's going to see me in all my poverty ridden glory.

"This isn't so bad," he says to me as Drakin pulls the car to a stop alongside the curb in front of my landlady's house.

"That's not mine," I say sheepishly, pointing out the converted two-story shed to the side. "That is."

"Ah," he replies, his tone flat as he tries to hide his obvious disgust for my living conditions. "Top or bottom floor?"

"Top," I say, hanging my head with shame.

"Well, at least it's not the bottom."

"You don't have to come in," I tell him in a rush as he opens his door. "The ride was more than enough, thank you."

He doesn't acknowledge my offer. Instead, he exits the car without a word, stopping to tell Drakin something I can't quite make out before coming around to open my door for me. I take his offered hand, stepping out of the car onto the street.

Thankfully, the usual smell of piss and rotten garbage seems less pungent today. Probably because it's just after sunrise and the sun hasn't had a chance to heat things up yet. It's always worse in the late afternoon, after all of the garbage and urine from the squatters occupying the surrounding vacant houses has marinated all day.

We walk in silence up the rickety wooden steps that lead up the side of the building to my apartment. As we reach the door, I can hear Samuel growl behind me as I turn the knob. "What?" I ask him over my shoulder as we step inside.

"There's no lock on your door," he grumbles behind me as he closes, then reopens, then closes the door again.

"There's a chain, but I can't exactly put it in place when

I leave for the day." I gesture to the rusted chain lock dangling from a screw in the doorframe. "When I'm home, I keep that on and put that piece of wood under the doorknob. Plus, I keep a bat next to my bed."

Samuel snubs his nose at the 2x4 propped up against the wall next to the door. I don't know why, but his discomfort and annoyance at my little makeshift home security system makes me giggle just a bit. It's obvious he has never been poor a day in his life, and to witness him seeing how the other side lives is more than a little entertaining.

I walk over to the bed and grab a clean pair of pajamas from the plastic tub I am currently using as a dresser. Samuel, scowl still firmly in place, walks around the room, which takes him all of about five seconds to do. I'm not sure why, but I turn my back to him as I pull my dress over my head and put on my pajamas. It's silly, I know, considering he has seen me naked twice now. For some reason, though, this seems different.

"What are you wearing?" The tone of his question matches his sour expression.

"My pajamas," I answer over my shoulder as I pull the faded blue t-shirt over my head. "Why?"

"You sleep in *that*?"

"Yes," I giggle as I pull up my favorite pair of sleep shorts, turning back to face him as I adjust them at my waist. "Again, why?"

"Take it off." It's a command, not a question.

I tilt my head at him quizzically. "Ummm, noooo," I tell him.

He pinches the bridge of his nose, and sighs loudly in exasperation. "I wasn't asking, woman. Take. It. Off."

The way he orders me to undress triggers something inside me. I feel my hands start to tremble. My knees almost give way beneath me. My anger at his demand is the only thing that keeps me upright. "No."

"You can either take it off, Seraphine," he says as he stalks towards me, his rage again glowing in his eyes, "or I can rip it off. Your choice."

"That's not a choice," I say, taking a step backward to keep some distance between us. Reaching behind me, I feel for the bat I keep propped beside my bed.

"I agreed to stay here with you, not realizing exactly what I would be compromising to do so," he barks at me, gesturing around us at the state of my meager apartment. "You *will* give me this."

The bile burned the back of my already raw throat. The hand behind my back wraps around the bat, prepared to swing if he takes another step. The fingers of my free hand grip the hem of my shirt tightly as if they will be enough to stop him if he tries to rip it away. Suddenly, I feel like a tiny kitten in a dog fighting ring, but I will not go down so easily. Not this time.

Samuel takes a step forward and I spring into action, swinging the bat around in a desperate attempt to keep him from making good on his promise. He catches the bat in his hand as if it were an annoying bug, holding it midair without letting it go. He looks at the bat, then back to me with an unreadable expression. Using the bat, he pulls me forward so that I crash into his chest. I stumble forward, almost falling over my own feet. Dropping the bat, he wraps his arms around me before I completely lose all balance.

"Why?" I choke out in a whisper around the lump in my throat.

"Why not?" he growls. "Fucking tell me."

"No," I whimper, trying my damnedest not to break down into a sobbing mess in his arms.

"Oh, fuck this." Before I have a chance to process what he is doing, Samuel lifts me up and tosses me on the bed as if I weigh nothing at all to him.

I bounce on the lumpy old mattress, unable to sit up before he is on top of me. He pins both of my wrists at my sides and presses me down with his body, rendering me completely immobile. I struggle and fight against him to no avail.

Samuel stretches my arms above my head on the mattress. He shifts his weight slightly, pushing my knees open with his. He gathers my wrists into one hand, shoving the other down the front of my shorts before plunging two fingers inside me. My back arches off the bed at the sudden intrusion.

I open my mouth to cry out in protest. Insead, a deep moan comes out. He curls his fingers inside me, hitting just the right spot to turn me into a quivering mess of need. My breath starts coming in short, ragged pants as I feel myself quickly nearing what will no doubt be another earth shattering climax. All the while, Samuel stares down at me with nothing but pure hatred in his dark brown eyes.

The familiar tingle of release builds in my core. My climax is so close, I can feel the sparks about to explode from every inch of m y skin. However, just before I fall over the edge into that abyss of pure ecstasy, Samuel removes his fingers and starts drawing slow, lazy circles around my aching clit without touching it directly.

Around and around, his fingers continue their torturous route, touching me everywhere except where I need them to. "Samuel, please." I beg.

"Tell me why," he demands, his voice strained, as if he is also trying to hold something inside himself at bay.

I shake my head violently from side to side, not trusting my own voice not to crack at this moment. Samuel growls through gritted teeth as he slams his fingers inside me again. As before, he brings me just to the edge before removing himself and torturing me again by tracing circles around my now throbbing clit.

Hot tears burn my cheeks as they stream down my face. My jaw aches from clinching so tightly to stop myself from telling him everything I know will send him running away from me and never looking back. My head spins from the need to release and subsequent continued denial of that release. It feels like hours, days, weeks have passed with him on top of me like this. I feel the edges of my resolve starting to crack when he removes his fingers for a fourth time, leaning down to whisper in my ear this time.

"I have all of human existence to do this, woman," he breathes into my ear. "I have tasted the paradise between your legs, and I want to spend eternity inside of you. Tell me why you are denying me what I have already claimed as mine." Exhaustion and frustration burn my lungs. I know I can't fight him anymore. I know he will leave when he knows what I am, what I was, and what I always will be.

"You are mine, Seraphine," he rasps, his fingers barely brushing against my tender, swollen clit.

Somehow, I manage to choke out a single question. "Forever?"

"Forfuckingever." With this, Samuel presses down on my clit and slams his lips to mine simultaneously.

My entire world shatters around me into a million brightly burning stars. My back bows and arches, almost breaking me in half. Wave after wave rolls through me like the sea in the midst of a turbulent storm. I feel as if I am both flying and falling at the same time. Never have I felt so powerful and powerless before. Samuel holds me to him, crushing my lips to his as I ride out the force of my orgasm. All too quickly, however, I feel myself crashing back to earth. I turn my face away from his, burying my head in the crook of his neck. Sobs rip through me as I finally break down.

He holds me through this, as well.

FIFTEEN

SAMUEL

I can't remember the last time I fell asleep fully dressed. Nor can I remember the last time I had blue balls. Now that I think about it, I don't recall ever having blue balls before today. However, laying here on this horrible excuse for a mattress as Seraphine sleeps soundly with her head resting on my chest, the ache in my testicals infuriates me.

No one has ever defied me the way she does. No one has ever denied me the way I *allowed* her to today. I am the goddamn King of Hell. No one has ever said no to me and lived to tell about it. No one but her.

The thought fills me with an emotion I am not sure how to describe. Rage doesn't feel adequate. This is more than that, but also different. I am just as angry with myself as I am with her. But something inside her broke this morning. Something I am certain she has not let anyone see for a very long time. With that, something inside myself broke with it. Something cracked wide open, and I am not sure if I can ever close this gaping hole again.

I shake my head to clear the questions starting to build up inside my mind. I am not ready to confront this new emotion right now. No, right now all I want is to drain myself inside her and get the fuck out of this shithole. Not necessarily in that order. Seriously, how does she manage to survive in such conditions? The money I paid her to sit in an empty room last week alone was more than enough to pay for a year in a much better place than this. Why would anyone choose to stay here if they had the means to leave?

She did have the means, didn't she? I remember Eve mentioning something about her being behind on her rent, but surely I paid her enough to get caught up and still have some left over to at least buy a proper bed to sleep on. Did she seriously spend it all on those people from the lot?

Looking around the single room of her apartment, I would venture to say yes. What kind of person does that? She is basically homeless herself, but chooses to spend whatever money she makes on *them*. Why?

Seraphine groans in her sleep, rolling to her other side away from me and curing up into a tiny ball on my arm. I pull the tattered blanket up to her shoulders as I carefully slip my arm from under her. She snuggles into the covers and sighs contentedly. I manage to ease myself out of the bed, if that's what she insists this thing is, without waking her. I barely fit within the makeshift walls of her bathroom to relieve myself.

Walking back into the singular room that encompasses her entire life, I take the opportunity to watch her as she sleeps. She looks more peaceful than I think I have ever seen her in the short time we have known each other. When she is awake, you can see the weight she carries around with her in the storm that continually rages inside her eyes. Now that she is asleep, however, the storm and the sea are calm. With her white blonde hair fanned out around her beautiful face, she looks every bit the angel her name suggests she is.

I have never felt an ounce of physical pain once since my creation. A blessing God gave the entirety of the Heavenly Host. A blessing that became a curse after I was cast out. Being numb for an eternity has made me insensitive in ways other than just the physical. However, as I watch Seraphine in her slumber, my chest aches for her.

Turning away from the bed, I rub at the dull pain in my sternum with my fist. It was probably nothing, anyway. Looking at my watch, I realize it's been at least a day since I've eaten anything. Perhaps that is the cause for this feeling in the pit of my stomach. I don't get hungry, nor do I actually need food to survive. But I have found the eating of food to be one of the great pleasures of this life, and try to have at least one meal a day to maintain my mortal facade.

A quick scan of the small cart Seraphine uses for a kitchen shows nothing to eat in sight, though. I open the small minifridge only to find coffee and a half eaten cup of yogurt. No wonder she is so thin.

For some reason, the lack of basic provisions makes me even more angry than I already was at her living situation. No food in the kitchen, no locks on the door, no real furniture, and hardly any clothes. How in the fuck has she managed to survive like this? Well, this changes today. No matter how much she protests, she will not be spending another night in this slum.

Headlights from an approaching car shine through the

small holes in the curtains covering the only window of the apartment. The light briefly illuminates something in the corner I hadn't noticed before. A large canvas is propped against the empty wall, turned so that only the back is facing out. I walk over to the canvas, carefully turning it forward to examine it.

It's a painting. A rather large painting, to be exact. The top of the canvas is as tall as my hips and equally as wide. In the dim light, it's hard to make out exactly what the painting is of, but I can tell from the smell of freshly dried acrylic that it must be relatively new. Black and red streaks cover the canvas in an almost abstract-like fashion. Even in the darkness, I can tell it is exquisite.

Another car passes, and I notice there are two more paintings behind this one; all of which are turned to face the wall. I pull them out one by one as quietly as possible, checking over my shoulder that I am not caught snooping. Not that I would care in the least if I was. The second painting I discover has much lighter colors, making it easier to see in the low light. It's of a simple looking white frame house with what appears to be a small vineyard growing beside it. In the distance, there is a dark red barn and two white rocking chairs on the front porch of the house. The painting reminds me of a more modern Norman Rockwell type of scene, with its slice-of-Americana feel to it. A stark contrast to the first and obviously most recent picture.

The third painting is of a nun, of all things. She is in profile, bent down covering a junkie who looks nearly passed out in a gutter in some back alley somewhere. It's hard to make out at first, but there is something familiar about the junkie in the painting. It's obviously a woman, but she is covered in so much filth I can't make out very many details about her. Her hair is stringy and matted with mud in some places. The collar of her shirt is ripped so far down, one of her breasts is exposed. There is blood trickling down the gutter from under the blanket, though one can't determine from which part of the girl's body it is coming from. It's not hard to guess, though.

I note the purplish bruising in the bends of the girl's elbows on the visible arm. Must have been heroine. The color of the girl's eyes are lost in the shadows of her sunken face, but something about them calls to me. I can't put my finger on it, but I am certain I have seen this woman before somewhere. After an eternity, however, many of the faces I have seen all blend together over the many years.

The nun's face is mostly shielded by her habit as she leans down over the girl. The only piece of her rich mahogany skin that is showing is the hand as she pulls the gray utility blanket around the girl. Her fingers are slender and bony with age, reminding me of a drawing of a witch's hand I saw in a children's book once. Her knuckles look crooked with arthritis, but even this small glimpse shows there is kindness in her touch.

"Sister Margaret." I swing around to see Seraphine sitting upright on the bed, hugging her knees to her chest. "Her name is Sister Margaret."

I hold my breath as Seraphine stares through me at the painting, silently urging her to continue. The haze of memory clouds her features. Whatever thoughts she is lost in are not pleasant ones.

"I painted that the first week I was in rehab." She swipes at her cheeks, wiping away tears I cannot see in this darkness. "That was close to a year ago. This was the last day I woke up in a gutter with a needle in my arm."

Her revelation floors me, but also answers the question as to why the woman in the painting seemed so familiar. The woman is my Seraphine. She is the broken and bleeding junkie the nun was covering with a blanket.

"I don't remember much from that day, but when I woke up in that alley, all I could see was Sister Margaret standing over me as she waited for the ambulance to come. Even after a few weeks in the hospital's rehab facility, all I could see when I closed my eyes was this scene replaying over and over again inside my head." She gestures at the painting. I look back over my shoulder at the painting, rubbing at the ache inside my chest again as it seems to grow, then back to her as she continues to stare blankly ahead. "She had taken care of me so many times before then, but this was the moment I knew if I didn't change, I was going to die in that gutter. Sooner rather than later."

I want nothing more than to crawl back into bed with her right now. I want to bury myself inside her and erase every memory of that night from her mind, if only for a brief moment in time. I want to hold her, to protect, and reassure her that everything is okay now and that I will never let her spend another minute of her life bleeding in an alley again. I do none of those things, though. I have lied to her enough by telling her she will be mine forever. Forever is such a long time; longer for me than it ever will be for her.

So, I simply stare at her through the veil of dim light filtering in from the streetlights outside, drinking in how beautiful she looks in her sadness. She wears it as if it were a garment made just for her. Normally, I delight in the misfortunes of the ones God chose over myself and my brothers. This time, however, I take no joy in her suffering. I do, however, appreciate the way she carries her burdens.

A sudden pounding on the door breaks through the stillness of the night. Seraphine recoils at the sound, her face scrunching up, as if she thought if she closed her eyes tight enough the visitor would simply stop existing. They didn't, though, and a moment later, they pounded on the door a second time.

"I know you are in there, angelito!" the grating voice of what sounded like an older Mexican woman yells from the other side of the door.

Seraphine groans, hugging her knees even more tightly to her as her head tilted upward towards the ceiling. "Great," she whispers, more to herself than to me. "Be right there, Rita!" she calls back to the woman as she scrambles up from the bed.

Seraphine digs through the plastic tub next to her bed, pulling out handfuls of clothes and dropping them on the mattress until she reaches the bottom. When she turns around, I notice a small stack of bills in her hand. It must be her rent money, and this woman is obviously her landlady. She flips on the lightswitch as she moves the wood board from under the doorknob and unhooks the flimsy chain lock.

The woman is muttering something under her breath in Spanish as Seraphine opens the door. Rita is a short woman with a pot belly and a leathery face carved with unforgiving wrinkles. I chuckle to myself when I finally get a good look at her. Rita Suárez and I know each other quite well.

"Good evening, Rita," Seraphine greets the woman with a warmer smile than the hag deserves.

"It will be a good evening if you have the rest of my money, angelito," Rita scowls, as she pushes her way into the room. "And who's lujo car is that out front? One of you drug dealer friends?"

"Rita Suárez," I say as her eyes meet mine.

"Señor Delvine," she gasps, then crosses herself. "Dios mío."

I wag my finger at her as I step closer. "You know that won't help you now, senorita. Not after the last time we met."

Seraphine looks between the two of us, her brow furrowed in obvious confusion. "You two know each other?"

"Rita and I met once," I explain, not taking my eyes off of the woman who's soul I took twenty years ago. "A long time ago."

"You have not aged, senor," she says, her tan skin now turning white as if she has just seen a ghost. Or the Devil.

My mouth curves in an evil smirk. "I wish I could say the same for you," I say as I circle around her like a hunter stalking its prey. "The years have not been as kind as you thought they would be, have they, senorita?"

"They have not," she says, her lips set in a sour line. "Nothing like what I was promised."

"What you were promised?" I laugh as I come around to face her. "You were never promised an easy life!" Rita opens her mouth to protest again, but I quiet her with a finger pressed over her lips. "If I were you, senorita, I would think very carefully about the next words that come out of your mouth. Let's not forget who and what I am."

Absolute terror clouds Rita's dark brown eyes. She swallows hard, but keeps her thoughts to herself as I remove my finger and take a step back. She nods her head in understanding before turning to leave.

"Um, don't you want the rent money I owe you?" Seraphine asks as Rita pushes past her in her haste to leave.

"No, she doesn't," I answer for her. "Because you no longer live here."

Both women whip their heads in my direction in unison, each with vastly different expressions on their faces. While Rita looks even more terrified than she already did, Seraphine's face is marred with murderous rage. Both reactions to my statement make my smile spread even wider across my face.

"Of course, senor," Rita replies meekly.

Seraphine doesn't say a word. She doesn't have to. Her eyes tell me exactly how pissed she is at me right now. I can't wait until she releases all of that rage in bed as soon as this old cunt is gone.

Rita turns to leave again, but I make sure to remind her of something I am certain she would rather forget. "Oh and, Rita?" She pauses with one foot already out the door, but doesn't turn back to face me. "I'll see you again. Soon." With that, she all but runs out the door while muttering a prayer in Spanish as she slams the door behind her, leaving me alone to face the wrath of my woman.

SIXTEEN

SERAPHINE

"What the fuck just happened?" I ask Samuel as soon as Rita slams the door as she leaves, saying something in Spanish that I don't understand. "How the fuck have you known my landlady when she's lived here for the better part of a decade and you just got here a week ago? And when in the absolute goddamn fuck did I agree to move out of my apartment?"

Samuel rolls his eyes as he turns away from me, huffing a laugh and loosening his tie as he strolls nonchalantly over to the bed. "How I know Rita is none of your business," he says, tossing his tie on the floor. "And you agreed to be mine the moment you let me bury myself in that juicy cunt of yours." He starts unbuttoning his shirt, still with his back to me. "I gave you more than enough chances to walk away and you didn't. Did you think I was joking? Or that I would be okay with you continuing to live in a shithole like this?"

"I *think* it's not your decision to make, despite the fact that I allowed you to fuck me!"

"Well," he chuckles, peeling his form fitting shirt from his body, and tossing it aside to join the discarded tie, "I guess you thought wrong."

My entire field of vision goes blood red with rage. I've been angry before at him, but nothing like this. I can feel the heat burning my face from the blood boiling in my veins. Of all the things he could have said to me, *telling* me that I have to move just because he can't handle the fact that I live in less than ideal conditions than he does was not something I was expecting. Fuck him for looking down his nose at the life I have fought so hard for. Fuck him for thinking that just because I let him put his dick inside me, then that gives him the right to tell me what to do and where to live. And fuck me for thinking there was anything more than a greedy, self-centered asshole lurking somewhere inside him.

"Get the fuck out of my apartment," I tell him in a deathly calm voice.

Samuel's barking laugh echoes off every wall in the apartment, booming loudly enough to shake the uncovered lightbulb hanging from the ceiling. He slaps his thigh as he doubles over, continuing to laugh as if I have just told the funniest joke he has ever heard in his life. I swallow down the angry lump in my throat, fighting off the tears threatening to fall from the corners of my eyes.

"I said, get the fuck out, Samuel," I repeat more firmly.

Samuel doesn't respond, his laughter starts to subside. He shakes his head as he undoes the buckle of his belt and unzips his trousers. He shoves the pants, along with his boxer briefs, to his ankles in one swift motion, kicking them aside as he finally turns back to face me. I sway slightly on my feet at the sight of his sculpted body, naked for the first time in front of me. Yes, he had seen me naked a few times in the short time we have known each other, but he had always remained clothed. Even when he was fucking me in his office less than twelve hours ago, he never took his clothes off.

"Oh, God," I whisper to myself.

Samuel's expression shifts instantly. His eyes darken, then begin to glow as red as the fiery infernos of Hell. His lips curl into an angry snarl, like a dog baring his teeth before a fight. "I told you before, woman," he says in a deceptively calm voice through gritted teeth, as he stalks towards me. "I am not your fucking God." He wraps his arms around my waist. I shove as hard as I can against his chest, beating my fists against his hard muscles until they ache. It doesn't even seem to register with him as he continues to carry me kicking and screaming over to the bed. "I am the fucking Devil. *Your* fucking Devil." He tosses me in the air and I land on the mattress, just like earlier. "And you will find no mercy with me."

"Fuck you!" I scream, scrambling to try to pull myself up before he has a chance to overpower me again.

Samuel throws his head back in laughter. "Oh, my sweet, precious Seraphine," he says in a sickeningly sweet tone, his dark red eyes meeting mine, pinning me in place with their hypnotic glow. "You should have chosen your words more carefully."

Before I have a chance to react, Samuel climbs on top of me and pushes me back down on the mattress. He pushes my legs open with his knees easily, settling between my thighs as if he belonged there. The way we fit together, maybe he does.

I feel his erection through the thin fabric of my shorts. My body instantly responds, recalling the memory of how he felt as he moved inside me. I try to buck him off of me, but the friction it causes only makes things worse. Wrapping my arms around his neck for leverage, I'm not even sure anymore if I am trying to push him off of me or pull him closer.

We both struggle for control of the other, neither of us willing to give in, but also neither of us wanting this to stop either. Our mouths crash together so hard, our teeth clink against each other. He invades my mouth with his tongue. Or do I willingly let him in? My head is such a clouded mess of confusion, I'm not sure anymore.

Samuel's lips move across my jawline, tracing up the side of my throat before he nips at the lobe of my ear. "Take off your clothes." he rasps in my ear, sounding as if he has a beast inside him he is desperately trying to keep at bay.

"I'm staying in my apartment," I growl into his ear.

He rocks his hips forward, his hard cock rubbing against my swollen clit through my clothes. I let out a long, agonizing moan at the sensation. "Take off your clothes, woman, and I will give you what you need."

He's resorted to bargaining. The last attempt of a desperate man. I dig my nails into his back, raking them down and grabbing his ass. I pull him forward as I spread my legs wider. "Let me keep my apartment, and I'll take off my clothes."

Samuel's head rears back as he lets loose a deafening

roar. The entire room shakes, and he sinks his teeth into my shoulder. A trickle of warm blood runs down my chest, between the valley of my tits.

"Fine," he grumbles in my ear.

Before he has even finished speaking that one word, he is tearing at my clothes. He easily rips my shirt down the middle. He spreads the torn fabric open, tracing his tongue along the path of blood. He laps up every drop before turning his attention to my tits.

He cups a breast in one hand, covering the entire mound with his huge palm. His skin is rough in contrast to mine. I feel the calluses as he kneads and squeezes me. My hands tangle in his thick, black hair when he covers the opposite nipple with his mouth. His tongue lashes at the hard peak, the sensation sending jolts of electricity straight to my core. My hips buck wildly off the bed, grinding against him in a desperate attempt to find some kind of relief from the ache building inside me.

Samuel is true to his word, though. I find no mercy with him. He continues his torturous worship with my other breast, paying the same respects to it as he did the first. Sweat beads across my hot skin. My eyes roll back in my head, and intangible words fall in a garbled mess from my lips.

I am so wet right now. I can feel a spot beginning to form on my shorts as Samuel's mouth begins to venture lower. "Your skin tastes like mother's milk," he rasps against my belly. His tongue dips briefly into my navel, tracing tiny circles that send a tingle all the way down my spine. "I have never seen skin so perfect in all my long years."

My head is lost in sensation as I feel his hands slide

along my rib cage. He hooks his thumbs inside the waist of my shorts, peeling them down my legs at an agonizingly slow pace. All the while, his lips caress my skin in such a tender way.

Samuel runs the tip of his tongue along my hip bone from one side to the other. He stops only for a brief moment to blow a short puff of his hot breath at the small tuft of pubic hair I leave. The feeling of his warm breath against my wet skin causes my back to arch again. I lift myself off the bed, allowing him the chance to fully remove my shorts. He tosses them aside without looking. I hear something break in the kitchen area. He must have knocked my mug off its nail.

I barely recognize the voice coming from my own lips as I moan with each inch he ventures lower down my body. Sweat soaks my skin, making my hair stick to my forehead and neck. I thrash against the bed, trying to angle myself in every way possible to get some kind of relief from the aching between my thighs. It's nothing less than torture as Samuel turns his attention to my thighs just before his mouth reaches my pussy.

"Please," I beg, my voice shaking.

"Not yet," he murmurs against my right thigh as he licks a trail down the inside of it.

"Please, Samuel, it hurts."

His answering huff of laughter tells me this was not going to yield the results I thought it might. "Good."

I claw at the thin sheets, hearing the fabric ripping in my grasp as I struggle. I've never wanted to come so badly before in my life. It feels like an explosion is building inside me, and there is nothing I can do to stop it. Every muscle in my body is tense to the point of pain. My toes are curled tightly against the soles of my feet. As Samuel gets to my knee, he lifts my leg and places it over his shoulder before turning his attention to the opposite thigh.

As he kisses and nips his way up the other leg, he simultaneously raises it as well, placing it over his other shoulder as he nears the apex of my thighs. I look down to see his glowing eyes staring back at me. "Watch," he commands. "And know that this is not God who does this to you."

Without breaking eye contact, his head dips lower. Again, he blows on my over sensitive skin. "You're so fucking wet," he whispers. He runs his tongue up my slit without parting it. "And you taste like honey." I feel as he slides one finger inside me, only to withdraw it almost immediately. I don't dare look away. I don't think I could if I wanted to. My eyes are locked on his as he brings his finger to his mouth and sucks the glistening wetness off of it.

Samuel closes his eyes briefly, moaning in satisfaction as he licks his finger clean. "Delicious." His head lowers again, but his eyes remain on mine. "Such a pretty pussy," he whispers, and I am not sure if he is talking to himself or to me. He sweeps his tongue across my skin again, this time parting my lips slightly but still not touching me where I need him to.

"Please, Samuel," I beg again, tangling my fingers in his thick black hair. I try to push his head lower, try to force him where I desperately need him to go, but it's like a child trying to push a boulder.

Samuel laughs at my futile attempts to get what I need

from him. "Are you aching, woman?" he asks in a sickeningly sweet tone.

I nod furiously, unable to speak at this point. Everything inside of me is wound so tight, I feel like I might explode at the slightest touch. A touch he refuses to give me. I dig my nails into his scalp, certain I feel blood trickling down my hand. Samuel simply laughs again, like he feels nothing at all as I claw at him. "Please," I beg, my voice thin and strained at this point. "Please, I can't take any more."

Samuel's thumb gently strokes the small patch of hair just above my slit as he watches me. "You are so beautiful when you are under me, begging for that which only I can give you." He places a chaste kiss to my mound, then plunges his tongue into me.

My eyes rolled back into my head, finally breaking the hypnotic spell his glowing red eyes had on me. My fingers tighten in his hair, no doubt taking a few strands with them. If I didn't know any better, I would think my entire body lifts off the bed, suspending me in mid air as he drags his tongue from bottom to top.

He devours me as if he is starving and I am his chosen meal. Each movement of his skilled tongue hits me in just the right way, bringing me closer to the edge I was already so close to. My head thrashes wildly against the mattress. Blood rushes in my ears, making the wet sounds as he licks every drop sound muted and far away.

"Do you have any idea what this pussy does to me?" He breathes, running his tongue in tiny circles around my clit. "You are the nectar that gives me life." I mewl and whimper, completely lost to the pleasure he gives me. "I have tasted every star in the Heavens, and none of them compare to you."

With this, Samuel slips two fingers, then a third into me with ease. He gives my clit a final flick of his tongue. "Come for me, Seraphine. Let your grace rain down onto me."

With those words, I shatter into a million fragments of myself. The entire world fades away in an instant, leaving only the two of us behind. Samuel pumps his fingers inside me, curling them slightly and hitting just the right spot to send me soaring all over again. Waves of pleasure crash into me like the ocean crashing mercilessly against the shore. Right when I think I am about to come back down to Earth, Samuel licks me again and keeps me in the stratosphere.

It feels like a lifetime has passed before he finally withdraws his fingers from inside me. I drag deep gulps of air into my burning lungs, thankful for a reprieve from the unending orgasm he just gave me. Samuel pushes himself back on his knees, but keeps my legs on his shoulders. Leaning forward again, he folds me in half and slams into me without any warning.

I let loose a long, throaty moan from somewhere deep inside me. The cliff Samuel threw me off of only moments ago is once again fast approaching. The room echoes the sound of his skin against mine as he pounds into me. I claw at his back, no doubt leaving more than a few marks across his skin.

"You didn't think we were done, did you?" he chuckles between strained breaths. "I will never be done with you, Seraphine. Not now. Not fucking ever."

He picks up the rhythm, slamming into me again and

again. With each thrust, he pushes himself deeper inside me, fighting against my tight and still trembling walls until I feel him bumping against my cervix. The room is filled with the sounds and smells of our lovemaking, if this is what you can call it.

Can you, though? This isn't love. This can't be. From the moment I first met Samuel, I have hated everything about him. I hate everything he stands for. His wealth and privilege. His Condescension and arrogance. His commands, his wrath, his entire existence. How can love even be a thought to me in this moment when I know that when the sun rises again, I will still hate so much of who he is?

"Stay with me, Seraphine," he whispers tenderly in my ear. His words are such a sharp contrast to everything about him sometimes. More and more, I find myself questioning what I have been so certain I knew before.

Samuel suddenly shifts slightly, angling himself in a way that pushes every other thought from my mind. "Stay with me," he repeats, trailing soft kisses along the edge of my jaw before claiming my lips.

He moves inside me ferociously while kissing me with such care. Lowering himself down on his elbows, he cups my face, stroking my flushed cheeks with his thumbs. My nails loosen their grip on his back as I hold him. In this moment, something inside both of us changes. Whether or not he feels it too, I am not sure. But God and the Devil both know I do.

Breaking our kiss, I tilt my head back as I feel another orgasm building in my core. My mouth falls open in a silent scream. Samuel reaches between us and massages my tender and swollen clit.

"Are you with me?" he asks.

With my eyes screwed shut, I nod once, completely unable to form a single word right now. Samuel doesn't respond. I feel his cock swelling inside me before I am filled with a familiar warmth. He buries his face between my breasts as he pours every drop of himself inside me. The feeling of his hot cum spilling out of me sends me flying over the edge once again.

All of the stars in the sky dance in front of my eyes as I spiral downward into the abyss of my orgasm. My skin burns and freezes all at once. Every possible sensation washes over me at the same time. Through all of it, Samuel is there holding me, possessing me, and pulling me down into the very depths of Hell.

As my soul slowly starts to find its way back to my body, Samuel collapses beside me. His chest heaves up and down with heavy breaths as he stares up at the stained ceiling. The red glow dims in his eyes, the dark haze of thought replacing the fiery embers. Sleep weighs heavy on my exhausted body, quickly pulling me under. I roll to my side away from him, shivering as the beads of sweat start to dry on my damp skin. As I feel myself succumbing to the darkness of a dreamless sleep, Samuel curls his body around mine. His arms wrap around my waist, hugging my back tightly to his chest. A faint smile tugs at the corners of my lips when I feel the little hairs on his chest tickling my sensitive skin. After a moment, the soft sounds of his snoring let me know he is asleep.

My eyes struggle to stay open, but I take this rare

opportunity to examine his bare skin. This is the first time he has been naked around me. I trace my fingers up the lines of the tattoos as they extend up his forearm. While I can't turn to see them now, I have noticed lines peeking from under the collar of his shirt. I assume these lines continue all the way up his biceps to his shoulders and neck, possibly even onto his back.

The lines become fussy as my heavy eyelids struggle to stay open. I open my mouth in a wide yawn as I snuggle deeper into his protective embrace. As I am drifting away into what I know will be a deep slumber, I notice something about his tattoos. A single thought crosses my mind before sleep takes me.

Those lines look a lot like feathers.

It feels like I've only just closed my eyes when the light coming through the tattered curtains starts to warm my face. I pinch my eyes closed, trying to fight off the morning for a few minutes longer. I stretch out my arm, feeling for Seraphine's body to pull back to me. She had stayed so close to me during the night. It felt good, having her nestled up against my chest. The strange ache in my chest seemed to disappear when she was close to me. Now, I didn't need to open my eyes to know she had moved away from my arms. The dull ache had returned, so I reached out to pull my relief back to me.

However, my hands were met with nothing but cold sheets. I cracked open my eyes, confirming she was not in the bed with me. For a moment, another new and unfamiliar emotion crept up my spine.

Fear.

I grabbed her pillow, pulling it to my face and inhaling her intoxicating scent that lingered on the fibers. Sweet florals and salty sea air. It was a scent I wish I could bottle so that I would never be without it again. Now, I feared this would be the last time I ever got high off the scent again.

A squeaking sound followed by the sound of water sputtering to a stop, pulls me from my melancholy thoughts. I roll over to see Seraphine wrapping a towel around herself as she steps out of the makeshift shower. Little drops of water splash against her skin as they drip from the ends of her white blonde hair. I note a few marks and bruises on her otherwise perfect, porcelain skin. I can't help but smile knowing it was me who marked her previously unmarked body. No one would ever be able to claim her in the way I have again.

"Good morning, sleepyhead," she says with a cheery smile when she notices me looking at her. "Was beginning to think you were going to sleep 'til noon."

"Usually, I don't sleep very much at all," I tell her as I pull myself upright, placing the pillow behind me and leaning against the wall that serves as her headboard. Looking down at my hands, I wrinkle my nose as I try to recall the last time I slept for more than a few hours. I have no biological need for sleep, but I have found my human body functions better when I am able to get a few hours every other day or so.

Seraphine unwraps the towel from her body, rewrapping it around her damp hair before pulling on a black thong and a pair of sinfully tight well-worn jeans. She doesn't bother with a bra, opting for a tight fitting white tank top. The hard buds of her nipples show through the thin fabric of the top. Seeing them reminds my cock of what it felt like to run my tongue over those nipples.

Seraphine freezes in place as her eyes notice the bulge

forming under the covers barely covering my lower half. I notice the muscles in her throat as she swallows, her eyes still locked on my hardening cock. Slipping my hand under the covers, I start stroking my length as I watch her. She rubs her thighs together, then suddenly shakes her head hard as if to clear it. She walks quickly to the small area set up with her microwave and minifridge, pretending to search for something to give her time to regain her composure.

"I would offer you some coffee, but you broke my only mug last night," she laughs awkwardly as she bends down to pick up the fragments of the shattered cup off the floor.

"I think I would rather have something else for breakfast instead," I smirk at her, throwing the covers aside. She glances over her shoulder at me, rolling her eyes at me, but doesn't fully turn around to look at me.

"I have shit to do today, Smauel," she says. "You're welcome to take a shower before you head out, but I would give it about an hour to let the water heat back up. Takes a while." She drops the pieces of glass into the trash, grabbing the broom next to the trash can. She starts sweeping up the pieces that are too small to gather by hand. "Just make sure when you leave, the door closes all the way. The latch sometimes doesn't like to catch so you may have to jiggle it a little or else it will swing back open when the wind blows it."

Wait. What? My hand stops moving mid stroke. "I'm sorry, but I'm a bit confused. Neither of us have to be at the club until later this afternoon. Why would we be leaving now?"

"*We* are not leaving. *I* am leaving because I have errands to run before work. *You* are welcome to stay here for as long as you want. Fair warning, though. It starts getting a bit loud around midday. The house across the street?" I nod, vaguely recalling a few vacant houses with boarded up windows as we drove past last night. "The guy that stays there sells stolen car radios out of the garage. Installs them, too. By two, that yard will be filled with cars using their systems to measure dicks with. Best to be out of here by then if you value your eardrums."

Swinging my legs over the edge of the mattress, I grab my discarded pants off the floor. I don't bother with my underwear. The entire suit is getting burned when I get back to my apartment anyway after spending the night on this peeling linoleum floor. But I can't exactly go the entire way home completely naked, so I will have to make do until for now.

I yank my pants up with a little more force than is necessary, tucking my now flaccid cock down one side so as to not catch it in the zipper. "Didn't we agree last night you would be coming with me this morning?" I bark at her as I grab my shirt and slip it on as well.

"I never fucking agreed to that," she says, slamming her fist against her hip. "If I remember correctly, you agreed that I could stay here."

"I said you could keep your apartment. I never said anything about you continuing to live in it."

"Since when do you get to tell me where I can and cannot live?" she yells.

"Since I fucking claimed you!" Her apartment is so small, and the walls are so thin that my booming voice causes bits of dirt to shake free at the seams. The tiny particles float through the morning light that fills the room like some kind of white trash confetti.

Seraphine's eyes darkened, turning into a raging storm of gray. She looked me straight in the eyes, neither of us saying a single word as we both seethed. My own anger at her stubbornness churned in my chest. After a moment, she stamped her foot, turning on her heel and stomping out the door. The door slammed closed behind her, a final protest as she stormed out.

Dragging my hand down my face, I groan in frustration before following after her. Outside, she is already on the sidewalk, head down as she walks in the direction of the city. "Stop right there, woman!" I bark as I close the distance between us.

"Fuck off, asshole!" she screams back to me as she picks up the pace. Makes no difference, though. She could be sprinting and I would easily be able to catch up.

I grab her by the arm, spinning her around to face me. Out of the corner of my eye, I see movement from the house across the street. I'm too distracted, however, by Seraphine pushing and punching at me to be too concerned with whatever it is. I hear a car door open and close as Drakin steps out of the car where he has been waiting all night. He doesn't say a word and keeps his distance, knowing better than to insert himself into this.

"Let me go!" Seraphine yells in protest as she continues to fight me.

"Get in the fucking car, Seraphine," I command as I start to drag her, literally kicking and screaming, back towards the car.

"No!" She digs her heels into the concrete. I groan again

in frustration, debating picking her up and throwing her over my shoulder to get her in the goddamn car.

"Yo, Sera!" a voice yells from across the street, followed by the distinctive sound of a gun being cocked. "This motherfucker bothering you?"

"She's fine," I call over to the man standing in front of the house on the opposite side of the street.

"Wasn't asking you, bitch," he says as he approaches.

The stranger's gun is still at his side, but I know he is ready to shoot me in the head in the event he feels he needs to. It won't do much, other than some surface damage to my human body, but he doesn't know that. And I'm not exactly ready for Seraphine to find out, either.

I release her arm and she takes a step back. She is still fuming, but doesn't say anything to me or the stranger. I hear Darkin as he steps behind me, keeping a few feet between himself and the stranger. I turn my attention away from Seraphine once I'm sure she isn't going to run off anywhere while I address the man with the gun currently standing between us.

"Sir, I would advise you to walk away right now. This is between my woman and I." My voice is as calm and even as I can manage.

This stranger, a dark skinned guy with a white wife-beater and baggy jeans on. The blue rag hanging out of his pocket shows his gang affiliation. He's tall, but not as tall as I am, but tall enough. The muscles in his biceps twitch as he squares up with me. I could crush him with zero effort, but that doesn't mean he isn't a formidable looking guy.

"You messin' with Sera, then it involves me, too," he

says in that overly confident way that small-time gang members talk.

Drakin takes a step forward, but I hold up my hand without looking to signal him that I've got this under control. "Listen," I smirk at him, "I can assure that if you do not walk away right now, you will not enjoy the Hell I can send your pathetic soul to."

He eyes me up and down, weighing his options in his head. Based on the heavy scent of fear that suddenly floods my nostrils, I can assume he is not liking his odds. He doesn't back down, though. For a low-level gang banger, he seems to have some kind of moral code when it comes to Seraphine. The thought of what could be the reason why he feels the need to protect her sets my teeth on edge.

"It's fine, Ricky," Seraphine chimes in, her voice a drastic change from the rage-filled screaming a moment ago. "Just a misunderstanding."

Both mine and Ricky's heads snap to look back to look at her. Her demeanor is a complete 180 from what it was. Her eyes have softened, the raging storm turned calm once again. Ricky and I look back at each other, both of us standing down from the other with a look of total confusion on our faces.

"You sure you good, Sera?" Ricky asks, still not sure what the actual fuck is going on.

"Yeah," she reassures him with a half smile. The way he returns her friendly smile with one that clearly is more than friendly makes me want to rip his eyes out of their socket. "Samuel, this is Ricky. Ricky keeps an eye on my place for me when he can."

"And my boys keep an eye on it when I can't," Ricky

says proudly as he extends his hand for me to shake. "Least we can do for our girl."

"*Our* girl?" I ask, emphasizing his choice of adjective.

"Yeah," he continues. "Sera here looks after us. Making sure the ones on this block who don't have nothing are taking care of. A few weeks ago, she patched up Marco when that dumbass cut himself installing a system in some fat cat's Benz."

"Why am I not surprised?" I ask, more to myself than to him.

"Yeah. Everyone around here knows not to fuck with Sera or they will have me to deal with." Ricky looks proud of himself for his unorthodox protection plan for Seraphine. I glance over to Seraphine, who is looking down at her feet sheepishly.

After a few seconds of awkward silence, Seraphine walks back towards the car. Drakin steps aside to let her pass, nodding at me before following behind her. He opens the back door and helps her climb into the car before closing the door again.

I turn my attention back to Ricky once she is safely in the car. "She isn't coming back for a while."

"Good. Girl like her doesn't deserve to live in a place like this."

"I agree."

"I'll keep an eye on her place 'til you're done with her."

"With any luck, that won't be for a long time," I chuckle. Ricky remains stone-faced.

"With any luck, my boys and I won't need to hunt your rich ass down when we both know what's coming comes."

He glares up at me, daring me to tell him differently. I

don't argue with his assessment of the situation, though. We both know this thing with Seraphine and I isn't going to end with a ring. It can't. She's mortal. And I am the Devil. No use trying to deny it.

I give him a curt nod, acknowledging his threat. Ricky turns without another word, tucking the gun back into the waist of his jeans as he disappears back inside the house he came from. I hear the muffled sounds of rap music kick on and the grinding sound of tools working. I don't think Ricky and I will be exchanging Christmas cards any time soon, but I do respect the guy.

Walking towards the car, an unsettling thought creeps into my mind. Sure, Seraphine may be waiting for me in the back seat, but that isn't what is bothering me. No, this nagging thought has to do with what happened last night. I did something I have never done in all the time I have been walking this earth. Something I didn't even think I was capable of doing.

I compromised.

I don't know why I did it. I am always the one who holds all of the proverbial cards. When there is something I want, I get it. Money, sex, souls; anything and everything at all. When what I want involves another person, they either agree to my terms or I find someone else who will.

No bargaining.

No questions.

No exceptions.

It's the way things have always been for as long as I can remember. And my memory stretches longer than anyone on this God forsaken rock can even fathom. However, last night, as I was buried inside her, Seraphine was able to make me do something I have never done. I compromised.

The thought of how much power she wields over me is...unsettling, at the very least. I gave in to her demands to keep her apartment, barely even putting up a fight over the matter. Had it been anyone else, I would have walked straight out of the room. Mid fuck or not, that would have been the end of everything with them. Not her, though.

It's not the first time either. I find myself more concerned with how my choices will affect the way she looks at me. More and more, she has invaded every facet of my life. I am the goddamn Devil, yet she is the one making all the deals.

Opening the door to the car, I slide into the backseat next to her. I turn to stare out the window without so much as acknowledging her presence beside me. The best thing for the both of us would be for me to tell her to get out and the both of us go our separate ways. I could easily sell the club for a nice profit by the end of the day. We would be free of each other, never to cross paths again. The thought of not having her in my bed every night, though, would be like living in my own personal Hell. I've tasted the waters of Heaven, and they didn't taste nearly as sweet as her pussy.

"Why did you change your mind?" I ask without looking at her.

There is a heavy silence between us as I wait for her answer. I glance at her out of the corner of my eye, hoping she doesn't notice. She tilts her head to the side, carefully considering her words before she speaks. When she finally does, her response floors me.

"You said *my*," she finally says, her voice low but certain.

My head snaps in her direction, not fully understanding what she meant. "What?"

"You said *my*," she repeats, answering by not really answering my question. "When you were speaking to Ricky. You said *my* woman. No one has ever called me theirs before."

Her head is still tilted away from me, a small smile playing on the corners of her lips. I want nothing more than to kiss those lips right now. I settle for placing my hand on her knee, drinking in her beauty in this rare moment of serenity and calm.

"I want to take you somewhere."

"Ok," she agrees.

I settle back in the seat, my hand still on her knee, relaxing a little after a tumultuous morning. I am still not sure what is happening to me, but I am at least a little more at ease with it. I can't help but chuckle softly to myself as the irony of it all. Even without arguing, she has still managed to make me compromise and show her something I had never intended her to see until I was out of her life.

I am the goddamn Devil, yet she is the one making all the deals.

EIGHTEEN

Pulling up to the shelter, I wasn't expecting to see this much progress had been made. After a little research, I learned the reason why Seraphine had moved everyone onto my property. The local shelter they all lived at had been closed due to lack of funding. Of course, lack of funding is usually code for wanting to spend the money allocated for one thing on something more appealing to the people in charge of writing the checks. A few phone calls and one meeting with the members of city council later, and the issue of funding was all cleared up. Amazing how quickly money can be found when the people in control are presented with a detailed folder of every sin they have committed since taking office. I also made a generous anonymous donation (and made a few deals) to ensure something like this never happens again.

Seraphine doesn't wait for Drakin or myself to open her door for her. She jumps out of the car as soon as it comes to a stop in front of the building. She runs right into the arms of an elderly woman with dark skin and a warm smile.

Immediately, I know this must be Sister Margaret from her painting. Stepping out of the car, I can't help but smile at the two women as they embrace. Tears stream down both of their faces, but neither of them says a word. After a few moments, Seraphine breaks away from the Sister and turns her gaze to me.

Tears sparkle like the sun reflecting off the waves in her eyes. Her smile shines more brightly than any star in the night sky, stretching across her face and illuminating every feature. My lips twitch up at the corners, her exuberant joy spanning the space between us to infect me as well. I can't recall a time I have ever felt this way at the sight of someone else's happiness. In this moment, however, I will burn the world to the ground just to ensure that the smile on her face never fades.

Sister Margaret says something to Seraphine I can't quite hear. She then gives her one of those reassuring pats on the hand like a grandmother gives a grandchild after imparting some much needed wisdom on them. A guy who looks no older than seventeen walks up and starts speaking to the Sister. He is wearing a bright yellow shirt with VOLUNTEER written in bold black letters across his chest. He motions over his shoulder to where a group of other teens are stacking donation boxes as he speaks. Margaret nods to the young man, then excuses herself from Seraphine before walking back inside to assist the rest of the volunteers.

Seraphine starts walking back over to where I am still waiting by the car. "Park the car, then go in and assist the Sister with whatever she may need help with," I instruct Drakin, my eyes not leaving Seraphine's as she approaches.

Stepping in close to me, Seraphine runs her palms up my chest. She wraps her arms around my neck, pushing herself up on her tiptoes to place a peck on my cheek before laying her head against my chest.

"Why didn't you tell me?" she says, her smile present even in her voice.

I shrug. "Would you have believed me even if I had?"

"Probably not," she giggles, lifting her head to look up at me with those big eyes. A man could get lost in those eyes. A Devil could, too. "How did you make all this happen so fast? I've been working for months to get the shelter reopened. You've done it in less than a week."

I raise one eyebrow as the corners of my lips twitch up in a wicked smirk. "Do you really want to know?"

Her brow knits together, her head turning to look at everyone inside unloading box after box of donations and supplies. She thinks silently about my question for a moment, then shakes her head. "No. I don't."

"Didn't think you would," I chuckle, giving her a kiss on top of her hair.

Slipping my hand into hers, I lead her inside so we can both take stock on the progress that has been made. Even though I had ensured a crew was called to take care of the major repairs needed for everything to be brought up to code, the shelter had been vacant for a few months so there was a lot of cleaning that still needed to be done. I smile as I see Eve walk by carrying a box of pots, wearing jeans and the same bright yellow shirt as the teens, only hers says VOLUNTEER LEADER instead. I don't think I have ever seen her wearing this much clothing in all the years since I found her. Nor have I ever seen her this happy.

"It's coming along pretty good, don't you think?" she says, pausing in front of us with a beaming smile.

"Eve, this is amazing!" Seraphine says, still taking it all in.

"Yeah, it's nice," Eve answers, looking at a group of volunteers leading a mom and her two young kids towards the hall. "Feels good to have this again."

"Have what again?" Seraphine asked, perplexed by Eve's comment.

"A purpose," Eve says. "Been a very long time since I had one."

"Well, Eve, my dear, God definitely smiled upon us all by sending you here," Sister Margaret says as she approaches from behind us. "It's truly been a blessing having you here."

I roll my eyes, knowing she can't see my face from where she is standing. God most certainly had nothing to do with the progress that has been made here. I, however, had everything to do with it.

Eve's already broad smile stretches even wider across her face, the whites of her teeth a stark contrast to the deep tan of her skin and long dark hair. There is something just hiding behind the happiness in her eyes, though. While I know she has found something she had long since lost here, the pain from being cast out still lingers just below the surface. While I wear my feelings for being wrongfully exiled out in the open, Eve doesn't show hers as openly. I still see it, though.

There is a brief awkward silence before Seraphine mercifully speaks. "Eve, do you want me to help you unpack some of this stuff?"

"Yes, please! There are so many boxes in the kitchen I still need to get to before dinner tonight."

The two women walk away down the long hallway towards what I can only assume is the kitchen and dining area of the shelter. I turn to face Margaret, who is glaring at me with a knowing smile on her face.

"You are very different from the men I am used to seeing my little cherub with."

I shrug nonchalantly, not sure if she means it as a compliment or insult, but don't say a word. Generally, I have no problem with members of the church. I have made more than a few deals with more than a few priests, bishops, backwoods pastors, and even a pope or two. Nuns, however, are a different breed. Most of the time, they justify their own sins as doing the Lord's work. Most of the ones I have met are more ruthless and violent than any gangster. I don't get that vibe from the Sister, but there is something about her I cannot quite place. Something familiar, as if I knew her in a previous life.

"You're very good for her."

I snort a laugh. "I am not good for anyone, Sister. Especially not her."

"Why would you think that?" I open my mouth to answer her, but she cuts me off before I can. "Walk with me, young man. These old bones aren't what they used to be, and I could use a rest in the garden."

Without waiting for me to offer, Margaret takes my arm and starts leading us to the back of the building and outside into a small courtyard.

The courtyard isn't impressive by any means. The fountain is crumbling and not functioning. There is only a single bench along the circular walkway that isn't broken. The weeds have completely taken over the flowerbeds, choking out the few plants and bushes that haven't been uprooted by years of neglect.

"This garden was my pride and joy when we first opened this shelter," Margaret says wistfully, looking around as if she can still see things as they once were. "Of course, back then, I was able to do a lot more here than I can now."

I help her ease down onto the bench, making sure it will hold her before fully letting go. I remain standing, hoping she will dismiss me now that I have helped her to her seat. "I will have a landscaping crew sent out tomorrow to ensure everything is restored to its former glory."

Her bolstering laugh surprises me. "You like throwing your money around, don't you?"

"Doesn't your church say that we should all help those who are less fortunate than we are?" I smirk down at her.

"I have a feeling, though, your help comes with a string attached. And that string is tied to my little cherub, isn't it?"

I clench my jaw at her implication. "She was...relentless about helping these people. To the point she was suffering herself. I couldn't allow that to continue. Though, it would seem, your God was willing to sacrifice her for them."

"My God had nothing to do with the kindness she showed these people," she smiles, realizing she has successfully hit a nerve with me. "You don't know much about her life before, do you?"

"I know enough."

"Yes, I believe you think that. But if Seraphine means

anything at all to you, then knowing where she came from should mean something to you as well." I swallow hard, then take a seat next to the Sister, silently urging her to continue.

She places a hand on my knee, her knotted fingers barely more than bones. Her dark skin is starting to gray in some places. She doesn't have much more time left in this world. While I could offer her more time in exchange for her soul, I don't. I can see in her warm brown eyes how tired she is. Margaret deserves a peaceful rest when her days come to an end.

"Don't you go thinking I am about to tell you some big secret or anything. Seraphine tells this story herself every now and again. Mostly to the young people who come in here messed up something horrible on whatever they have snorted or smoked or shot up into their veins. Too few of them, though, learn anything from her story. But I think you just might." She pats my knee the same way she patted Seraphine's hand earlier. "Have you seen her paintings yet?"

"A few of them," I nod. "This morning at her apartment."

"Then you've seen the one she painted of herself in that alley the day she decided to finally get clean." Again, I nod, not wanting to interrupt her. "That wasn't the first time I had picked my little cherub up out of that gutter, though. Thank God it was the last. She wouldn't have survived another night had she stayed out there on those streets any longer."

Sister Maragret's eyes get a faraway look in them as she recalls the past. "Seraphine had been living on the streets for a couple of years when I first met her. Her mother was on drugs, too. No idea where her father is. Not sure her mother even knew who he was. Probably for the best anyway, considering her mother was a prostitute on top of being a drug addict. According to Seraphine, she and her mother started using together when Seraphine was about fourteen years old."

Margaret adjusts her black skirt as a breeze passes through the courtyard. It's only September, but the air seems to already be getting cooler. I remove my coat, draping it around her shoulders. My fingers graze her skin as I adjust the coat around her frail shoulders. I can feel the cancer in her veins. The ability to feel sickness inside of someone is a gift I have perfected over the years. It's a little trick that has come in handy quite a few times in the past. This isn't any different. Sister Margaret is sicker than she lets on.

Covering her hand with mine, I take her pain away for a little while. No charge. Margaret smiles weakly, probably unaware she is smiling at all. Her entire body relaxes as the pain eases inside her body before she continues.

"I first met Seraphine when she was sixteen. She had been on the streets for a little over a year by then, selling her body to support her addiction. Oh, I knew there was something special about my little cherub from the first time I met her. Something tells me you know what I mean." The Sister nudges me with her elbow playfully.

"I do," I chuckle. "We didn't exactly hit it off right away, though."

"Sounds like my little cherub," she laughs, but it quickly turns into a hard cough. "Was the same for the first few years I knew her, too. That girl is as guarded as they come. You must be something special if she let you in as quickly as she did."

"I'm not so sure about that," I mumble under my breath.

"Why not?"

"Let's not act like you don't know, Sister. I am a bad man."

Margaret tosses her head back in laughter again, As if I have just told her the funniest joke she has ever heard. "You sound just like she did that day."

"What do you mean?"

"It was about a year ago when I found her in that alley. She was barely alive. Had a needle still hanging out of her arm, beat up, and bleeding from being passed around by some dealer she owed money to for Lord knows how many days."

My jaw clenches. "Names." They didn't know it yet, but they were all dead men.

"An *actual* bad man. Travis. I haven't seen him in a while, though. Heard he had to run off to the east coast after ripping off some gang members."

My nails dig into my palms. It doesn't hurt, but I can feel the skin breaking. I stand again, pushing my fists into my pockets to hide the blood before it starts to drip from my knuckles. When I get back to my penthouse in New York, it will be my mission to find this Travis guy and make sure he suffers as much as he made my woman suffer. Forever.

"You're not like him, ya know. Neither was she." Margaret's words snap me out of my murderous thoughts. "He was a bad man. He used everyone he knew, and didn't give two shits about the pain he inflicted on them."

"I've inflicted pain on a lot of people, too, Sister," I snarl. "More than you can even fathom."

Margaret's eyes harden in an instant. "Don't you ever assume what I can fathom, young man. I wasn't always a nun. I have seen things that would make your nightmares look like paradise."

I swallow hard, instantly regretting my words. "Forgive me, Sister," I nod, feeling more like a scolded child than the King of Hell right now. "I meant no disrespect."

Her eyes soften, but she doesn't address my apology. "I know you've done bad things in your life. Anyone who has spent more than five seconds with you can sense the bad things you have done. You have forgotten, though, *doing* bad and *being bad* are not the same thing."

A cold chill runs up my spine that has nothing to do with the wind. "I'm not sure I agree with you."

She shrugs her shoulders. "God does. So it doesn't really matter what you think."

This time when I roll my eyes, I don't care if she can see me. "God and I have not been on good terms in a very long time."

"Just because you turned your back on God doesn't mean God has turned their back on you. Sure, you've done bad things. By your account, a lot of bad things. All that bad still doesn't make you entirely bad. If I knew nothing else about you, what you have done for the people of this shelter is proof of that."

"One good deed does not undo a lifetime of wrong doings. Even your God would agree with that."

"If you say so, but the God I know wouldn't say that at all."

I swallow hard again, staring at a lone white flower pushing itself through a crack in the concrete walkway. "The God I know is much different from the one you know."

"God is the same to all of us. None of us are promised an easy life. The only difference between the God I know and the one you know is how we have reacted to the cards we were dealt." Margaret starts pushing herself up from the bench. I offer my hand, but she shakes her head as she stands without my help. "I am not so egotistical to think I will be able to change your mind about God, nor do I think I will convince you of how good you have been for my little cherub. All I will say is this." Her dull green eyes bore into me, as if she is looking into the depths of the soul I don't have. "If you truly are the man you believe you are, let her go now. She deserves that."

I nod once, and clear my throat. Margaret nods back, then turns and walks back inside. Looking down at the ground, her words repeat on a loop inside my head. Despite what the Sister thinks, I know I am no good for Seraphine. How can I be? Even this one gesture of kindness was made with selfish intent. Had I never met Seraphine, I never would have funded the reopening of this shelter. All of those families inside would still be out on the street, living and dying in the same gutter Margaret puller Seraphine out of.

Looking back over the countless years, I see only the evil I have brought to the lives of innumerable souls. Evil that I can never undo for them. And for what? What did I gain from damning all those souls? The Sister is definitely wrong about me. I am a bad man.

Like the little white flower growing at my feet, Seraphine clawed her way to the sun. Despite everything in her way, everything she has been through in her life, she defied the odds and blossomed. If she is to continue to grow and bloom, it cannot be in the dark shadow of my life. I have to walk away, for her sake, sooner rather than later.

CHAPTER

NINETEEN

SERAPHINE

S omething has changed. No. Not something. *He* has changed. And I'm still not sure if it's for the better or not.

In the weeks since the shelter reopened, I've noticed a shift in Samuel. He's become more withdrawn than he usually is. Not that he was exactly the most forthcoming person to begin with. Most of our conversations would end in an argument, followed my intense hate-fucking until one of us got our way. Lately, though, he barely speaks to me unless he is inside of me.

Sex seems to be the only thing that remains unchanged between us. Despite his change in demeanor, Samuel still stakes his claim on my body every chance he gets. If we are alone for more than five minutes, he finds some way to take me. I'm not complaining in the least, but I can tell there is something going on he is purposefully avoiding discussing with me.

His possessiveness has also kicked into overdrive. I haven't been allowed to go back to my apartment since the night he stayed over. When I asked about going back to retrieve some of my clothes and the few art supplies I have, I was told no. The next morning, I woke up to more than half of Samuel's massive walk-in closet filled with designer clothes in my size. I was pissed beyond measure, until I saw he had also converted the guest suite into an art studio for me. Never in my life had anyone done anything like this for me. I made sure to show my appreciation by sucking him dry.

Work has been interesting since everything happened between us, as well. Each night as soon as I arrive, Eve tells me my mystery man has booked me for the entire evening again. After the second week of him not showing, I stopped looking for him every time the door opened. It was never anyone other than one of the other girls coming to bring me food or to refill my drink. I still don't understand why someone would pay so much money for my company, only to stand me up night after night. However, it is nice that I no longer have to dance naked for horny men in order to pay my bills.

Samuel tells me constantly I don't need to work anymore. The topic is currently our biggest reason for arguing. I know he has the means to take care of me, but letting him pay for everything makes me feel...dirty. I compromised and let him take care of my rent, but I put my foot down about everything else. With the shelter open again, though, and him covering the biggest expense I have, at least I am able to put some cash away for emergencies. Or for when he decides he's tired of arguing with me and finally leaves.

I talked to Sister Margaret about this nagging feeling I

have in the back of my head, but she just laughed at me like she always does when I worry. Still, I can't fight the feeling that this change in Samuel means the end is closer than I care to think about. Even now, sitting beside him in the backseat of the car as Drakin drives us to Eden, Samuel feels like he is a million miles away from me.

As if sensing something is wrong, Samuel reaches across the seat and covers his hand with mine. I smile as I look over at him, but he continues to stare blankly out the window as we drive. I intertwine our fingers, squeezing his hand and hoping he gives me some kind of a sign everything between us is okay. The car comes to a stop in front of the club, though, and he jumps out almost as soon as Drakin cuts off the engine.

My hand suddenly feels ice cold in his absence. The chill spreads throughout my entire body. I curl my arms around myself, hugging myself tightly to fight against the cold, ominous feeling blooming in my chest. A second later, my door opens and Samuel offers his hand to help me out of the car. Reluctantly, I take his hand and step out onto the curb.

Once outside, the cool October night air hits me. I rub my arms, wishing I would have brought a sweater. Drakin hands me my backpack from the trunk as Samuel removes his jacket and wraps it around my shoulders.

"Should have listened to me," he smirks.

"About what?"

"When I told you to go put on a sweater."

I roll my eyes as I push my arms into the sleeves of the jacket. "Maybe if you would have suggested it more nicely, I would have listened," I say, giving him a saccharine sweet smile.

"No, you wouldn't have," he laughs, then presses his lips to my forehead.

For a moment, my anxiety melts away. Everything is right with the world, and the knot in the pit of my stomach loosens. Samuel takes my backpack from me, slips his hands into mine, and presses his forehead against mine. I breathe in his intoxicating scent. Sandalwood and smoke. The smell is as comforting to me as his arms when he holds me against his body at night when we sleep.

"We need to go inside," he whispers, his voice laced with the disappointment that we have to leave this moment behind.

"I know," I answer, squeezing my eyes closed to block out the rest of the world as much as possible.

Neither of us moves, wanting to stay in this bubble a little longer. We haven't had very many moments like this in the past few weeks. To the outside world, Samuel is so cold. However, in these brief moments with me, I see the man he hides away. I know he wouldn't agree with me, but he is not the devil he often calls himself.

The blaring sound of a passing car honking its horn pulls us both out of our own heads. I flinch and Samuel takes a step back away from me, letting my hands fall back to my sides. He clears his throat, the mask he wears slipping back into place before we enter Eden, and straightens his tie.

It's the new tie I bought him a few days ago. The deep red color reminded me of the glow I thought I saw in his eyes the night he saved me from being raped. It's not as fancy as the ties he normally wears, but I wanted to get him something with my own money to show him how much I appreciated everything he has done for me since we've met.

The knot in my stomach starts to tighten again as we make our way inside the club. The dim lights dance around the main room as the bass thumps from the speakers surrounding the stage. Charmaine is on the main stage finishing up her set while a few of the regulars throw bills at her feet. I look around for Eve, but she is nowhere in sight. *Odd.* Normally, she is waiting by the front door when I walk in to let me know my mystery man has booked me again for the night. I shrug it off, assuming she must be in the changing room waiting for me, but I can't shake this feeling that something isn't right.

I turn to look back at Samuel and say my goodbyes to him until my shift is over, only to find him staring up at the mirrored one-way glass of his office window that overlooks the main floor.

"I have a meeting tonight. I'll come and collect you as soon as I am finished," he says over the loud music without looking at me.

Bile rises in the back of my throat. I've seen the look he has in his eyes now many times before, usually when we are arguing and he is about to end it by fucking me into oblivion. I nod once before turning away, hoping I can make it back to the changing room before I start to cry. The little voice in the back of my head warns me this meeting that has suddenly come up has nothing to do with business.

Before I make it two steps, Samuel grabs my wrist and spins me back around to face him. He slams his lips against mine, devouring mine. There is a desperate passion in his kiss, as if he was kissing me for the last time. His lips did not soften as he kissed me. Instead, I could feel every inch of him hardening.

When he finally pulled back from me, my lips burned from his. His eyes were dark, but I could see the red glowing just beneath the deep brown color. I can feel the heat radiating from his skin, his entire body burning hot with rage.

"Samuel-"

"You are the soul I never knew I had, Seraphine," he whispers in my ear. Without another word, he turns and disappears up the stairs to his office.

I want to chase after him, make him tell me what the fuck is going on and what just happened. I decide against it though, opting to give him a few minutes to cool off before I try to talk to him. I make my way through the growing crowd to the changing room in the back, my head still reeling from his kiss. Samuel has always kissed me with a deep and resounding passion, but this was different.

Opening my locker, I hang my backpack on the peg inside and start rifling through it to find the outfit I had packed for tonight. I set it on a chair beside me before reaching down to unbutton my jeans. As I go to undress, I realize I am still wearing Samuel's jacket he gave me outside. I forgot to hand it back to him when we came inside.

Looking around the room, I still see no sign of Eve anywhere. She must still be at the shelter. Ever since it reopened, she has been spending a lot of time there helping the children and organizing a local group of teenagers who volunteer in the afternoons. Or perhaps she is who Samuel is meeting with in his office. Either way, I need to return

Samuel's jacket to him before I head to the VIP room for the night.

I walk out of the changing room and over to the stairs leading up to the second floor of the club. Before I take my first step up, I pause for a moment. The knot in my stomach tightens again, making me feel like I am about to vomit. I stare at the staircase while I try to slow my heart pounding behind my ribs. I'm not sure why I am so nervous about going up there to Samuel's office. At least once a night, I make my way up there after the club is closed. Usually so he can fuck me on the couch in his office before we go home for the night. Tonight, however, I have to force myself up the steps.

Standing in the hallway in front of his office door, I slip the jacket off and raise my hand to knock before letting myself in. He said he had a meeting, and I got the impression someone was already upstairs waiting on him when we arrived. I can hear Samuel's muffled voice coming from the other side of the door. I lower my hand, deciding to hang the jacket on the doorknob instead so as to not disturb his meeting.

I know I should go back downstairs, but my legs suddenly forget how to move. Samuel is talking, though I can't make out exactly what is being said. There is a pause, followed by laughter. A woman's laughter. A woman's laughter that I know I have heard before.

"Is this about that woman you've been fucking, Light Bringer?" the female voice laughs mockingly. "Is that why you have stayed here with them for as long as you have?"

My heart sinks all the way down into my toes. He's not having a meeting with Eve. The voice on the other side belongs to the woman I saw leaving his office the night Samuel first claimed me in his office.

"*That woman* is of no consequence, Havoc," Samuel's voice booms loud enough for me to hear each word clearly. "She has nothing to do with you and I."

That woman he's been fucking.

They are laughing. About me.

Hot tears burn streaks down my face as my entire world spirals out of control around me. I can hear the blood rushing in my ears, drowning out the music playing downstairs. The jacket falls from my hand and my knees feel as if they will buckle underneath me at any second. Pain, rage, and betrayal boil inside my now empty chest at what I am hearing. Everything inside me goes numb as those words echo inside my head.

I don't even realize what I am doing until my hand has already turned the knob. Barging into Samuel's office, I am not sure what I plan on saying to him. All I know is I need to hear it, I need to see it for myself to know this is real and not some kind of nightmare. Part of me hopes it is a nightmare, and I am going to wake up any second now beside him in our bed back at his apartment. As soon as I step inside, though, I know this is not a nightmare from which I can wake up from.

CHAPTER

TWENTY

SAMUEL

If I had the ability to stop time and live in this moment forever, I would. There is nothing I would not be willing to give, no one I would not be willing to kill to be able to hold her in my arms like this until forever's end. But the end is nigh, and there is nothing anyone can do to stop it. Not even me.

Seraphine smells like the ocean after a raging storm; like fresh air and salt water mixed together. With my forehead pressed against hers, I breathe in her scent as the world around us fades away. I want nothing more than to feel her warmth against my cold skin right now. Out here on this sidewalk, with the wind swirling around us, I feel more connected to her than I ever felt to anyone.

Of course, like everything else in this Godforsaken world, it doesn't last. The sound of a passing car blowing its horn for some unknown reason pulls us both out of our perfect little bubble. Seraphine flinches, something I have noticed she does quite often when she is startled. I take a step back away from her, reminding myself once again that this has to end soon.

I straighten my tie as I compose myself, running my fingers down the polyester fabric. She bought me this tie recently. I will never forget the sheepish and almost embarrassed look on her face as she handed me the little black box with a hand-knotted bow on it. I know she was worried I wouldn't care for the gift because it wasn't like the fine silk ties I normally wear. What she doesn't know is this is now my most prized possession. Of all the things I have ever owned, of all the things I can buy with my wealth, this cheap red tie means more to me than all of it. No matter what happens between us, I will treasure it for the rest of my days.

Holding the door open for her as we walk into Eden, I can already sense something is not as it should be. Stepping inside, the feeling only grows stronger. Scanning the room, nothing immediately catches my eye as being out of the ordinary. One of the girls, Charmaine I think her name is, is on the main stage dancing. A group of men are gathered around as they throw the entirety of their net worth at her feet. A few of the other girls are giving lap dances in the darkened corners of the main floor. The music is pounding and the waitresses are all carrying full trays of drinks to the waiting customers. We only opened an hour ago, but the place is already filling up with pathetic, desperate people looking to pay for the pleasure of a beautiful woman's company for the evening. Still, something is off. I can feel it in my bones.

"Sir," Drakin leans in to say so that I can hear him over

the loud music. "Security has informed me that you have a guest waiting for you in your office."

My eyes focus on the pane of mirrored glass above the bar that overlooks the club. I don't bother asking who is waiting up there for me. I can sense her even from down here. In my peripheral, I see Seraphine turning towards me before she leaves to change in the back.

"I have a meeting tonight," I tell her, not daring to take my eyes off the glass. "I'll come and collect you when I am finished."

I can see the color drain from her lovely face from the corner of my eye. She senses something is off. My clever woman. So intuitive. She has had to be in order to survive. It's one of the things I admire so much about her.

Seraphine nods once and turns to walk away, her head bowed with the weight of her sadness. I grab her wrist before she walks out of reach, spinning her around and crushing my lips to hers. A jolt of electricity sparks through my entire body as if awakening it from its slumber. I pour everything into this kiss; every emotion I have never felt, every word left unspoken, everything I know I will never get the chance to say to her ever again. I kiss her as if this is the last time I will ever do so. Because, in the depths of my being, I know that it is.

Seraphine starts to speak when I release her, but I cut her off before she can. "You are the soul I never knew I had, Seraphine," I whisper in her ear.

Before she has the chance to protest, I turn away and make my way up the stairs to my office. I can't stay with Seraphine any longer. I already put it off for longer than I should have for no other reason than my own selfishness.

To continue to do so would be a cruel punishment she does not deserve.

Opening the door to my office, I can feel the rage that has been building in my chest wrap itself around my throat like a python, choking me with anger. "Hello, Havoc." I say to her sharply, not bothering to hide my contempt at seeing her again. "Get the fuck out of my chair."

Havoc's jade-green eyes claw at me like an eagle's talons as she stares at me from behind my desk. Her full lips thin with anger as she rose from my chair and walked around the desk. "Nice to see you again, as well, Light Bringer," she says in a deceptively sweet voice that bordered on mockery.

Her tight leather pants hug the curves of her admittedly perfect ass to perfection. There was a time I would spend days worshiping her body, defiling her in the most unholy of ways. Now, however, the sight of her turns my stomach.

"What are you doing here?" I ask, not wanting to endure this interaction any longer than I have to.

"Can't I visit an old friend without a motive?" She feigns an innocence she has never possessed.

"No," I counter icily.

"You know why I have come here, Light Bringer."

"I do?"

"Yes. You have been here too long. Word on the street is you are going soft. Not a good look for you."

"I could not give any less of a shit about what anyone thinks of me," I tell her with a roll of my eyes, accentuating the annoyance I feel with my tone.

"You need to come back, Light Bringer," she says, lowering her tone to a sultry, seductive tone as she stalks towards me. "You don't belong here with these mortals. Deep down, you know I'm right."

I don't bother arguing with her. She's right. I don't belong amongst mortals. I belong in the shadows, where I have always lived. Since I have met Seraphine, though, I have spent more time in the company of humans than I ever have. No longer are my interactions with them limited to deals and handshakes when I take their souls.

From before the beginning of time, everything I have touched has been tainted by my darkness. Not even Heaven was spared from my curse. Eve, Drakin, every soul of this world and beyond has been forever corrupted. All because of me. I cannot let that happen to my woman. I also can't just leave her either. I want to make sure she is taken care of. She deserves at least that much.

"I will leave when I am good and ready to," I snap, pushing past Havoc to take my seat. "Not a single fucking second sooner."

Opening my laptop with one hand, I wave Havoc away with the other without looking back up to her. I open the browser and open my banking app. A few clicks later, Seraphine's bank account is significantly larger than it was when she woke up this morning. Havoc moves in my peripheral, I assume gathering her coat or bag or whatever the hell she brought in with her. I don't pay her any attention, making one final donation to the shelter which will ensure it is financially able to keep the doors open for the next ten years.

I sigh loudly in annoyance when I sense Havoc saunter up beside me. I turn in my chair to face her, ready to be done with this so I can leave before Seraphine notices. My jaw falls open when I see Havoc kneeling on the floor completely naked.

Her eyes burn with lust as she tentatively reaches forward, running her delicate fingers up my thighs. My breath catches in my throat. She keeps her eyes locked on mine as her hands continue working their way slowly upward. Her sharp manicured nails scrape against the fabric, brushing against my cock. I want to stop her, but I am too stunned to move.

She palms my crotch with one hand while the other begins to undo the gold buckle of my belt. I feel my dick twitch in response to her touch. Judging by the way her lips start to turn up at the corners, Havoc notices the effect she is having on my body as well.

"Stop,"I choke out, finally regaining my voice before she has the chance to fully free my aching cock from my pants.

Her hands still, but remain in place. "We both know you want this," she says, her voice like velvet as she speaks.

"No," I lie, pinching my eyes shut in an effort to regain control over my treacherous body.

Havoc lets out a barking laugh as she pushes herself to her feet. "Is this about that woman you've been fucking, Light Bringer?" She chuckles, straddling my legs and lowering herself onto my lap. My eyes fly open. "Is that why you have stayed here with them for as long as you have?"

"*That woman* is of no consequence, Havoc," I say as calmly as I possibly can.

My body vibrates with rage. I feel my skin burning and cracking at seams it doesn't have. It takes all of my strength to keep my true form from ripping my human one apart and burning this entire place to the ground. The only thing that keeps me from doing so is the fact that Seraphine is downstairs in the VIP room.

I grab Havoc's hips to shove her off of me. The sound of the door slamming suddenly startles me. My head snaps to the side, meeting a stormy sea of unshed tears in Seraphine's eyes. My breath leaves my lungs in a rush at the sight of her pained face.

Havoc stands without a word, staring at Seraphine and eyeing her up and down like a predator stalking its prey. I see her from the corner of my eye as she gathers her clothes from the pile she left them in, taking her sweet time getting dressed. She bends and moves even more provocatively than normal, putting on a show and flaunting physical perfection. Even though her eyes never leave mine, I know Havoc's show is more for Seraphine than for me. It's her sick way of taunting the woman she knows I care about.

Once she's dressed, Havoc starts to make her way to the door. Seraphine raises her hand to stop her. "No," she says, her voice devoid of all emotion as she continues to stare into the depths of my being with those soulful gray eyes. "I'm leaving. You can stay." She turns to leave, finally snapping me out of the frozen stupor I had been locked in.

"Seraphine, wait," I say, practically jumping out of my chair to stop her before she can escape through the door. "Let me explain."

I grab her wrist to stop her. She spins around, slapping me with all of her tiny might. The sound of her palm as it connects with the side of my face rings in my ears. My body remains rigid, though. My head does not snap to the side like you see in those cheesy movies when the heroine has finally had enough of the hero's bullshit.

But I am no hero. Judging from the expression on Seraphine's face, she is no damsel in distress either. I swallow hard around the words stuck in my throat, accepting my fate and bracing myself for the wrath she is about to unleash upon me.

"How could you do this to me?" she asks, her voice shaking as she tries to keep her composure.

I have never felt an ounce of human pain. Suffering is not a word in my vernacular. It is a human emotion, and one I have been spared from since my creation. Along with every other emotion. In this moment, however, looking into Seraphine's eyes rimmed with unshed tears that I caused, a deep resounding ache starts to spread throughout my entire body.

She looks at me, her tears betraying her as they begin slipping from the corners of her eyes and splashing on the pale skin of her cheeks. What I wouldn't give to be able to reach out right now and wipe those tears away. But I can't. I won't.

Her body trembles as she waits for an apology I cannot give her. The seconds tick by, turning slowly into minutes that feel like hours. Neither of us so much as blinks. Thankfully, Havoc stays silent as well, allowing me to drink in Seraphine's beauty one last time without interruption.

This is the moment I always knew would come. This is the moment she walks away from me. This is the moment I let her go.

In my mind, I can see her just as clearly as I see her standing before me right now. I see her with long silver hair, laying in a hospital room, clinging desperately to the life draining from her fragile body. I feel the pain growing in my chest as I watch over her in that depressingly white room, untouched by time as I see the only soul I have ever had dying from some disgusting disease. One day, she is going to die. There is nothing I can do to stop it, but I can set her free. I can let her think of me as the monster everyone assumes I am and live the rest of her life in peace and happiness.

"Aren't you going to say anything?" she chokes out, obviously trying not to let the sobs building in her chest rip through her in front of me.

"No," I whisper.

"Why not?"

"Because I am the Devil, Seraphine."

"Yeah," she scoffs, swiping the tears from her face. "I see that now."

She turns and yanks open the door, nearly ripping it off the hinges with the force. Her wrist slips from my grasp as she storms out of the room, slamming the door behind her. I swallow hard, my hand already missing the feel of her skin. She will hate me for the rest of her life now, but at least she will have a life worth living without me.

"Well," Havoc chuckles, breaking the heavy silence filling the room. "That was awkward. But at least now you can get back to what you do best."

I feel her hands running up my back. It feels like shards of glass digging into my flesh. She rests her hands on top of my shoulders, pushing herself on her toes to whisper in my ear from behind. "You don't belong with her."

Her words are my final breaking point. I let loose a

primal growl, spinning around and grabbing her by the throat. Lifting her off her feet, I walk her backwards until her back hits the wall. She groans, but I squeeze her throat tighter to make her shut up. I am done listening to the siren sound of her voice.

"How did you know about Seraphine?" I spit at her, my nostrils flaring with fury.

"M-M-Michael," she stammers out between struggling gasps of breath.

"Michael?" I repeat, my rage growing with the growing pain in my chest.

"Yes," she confirms. I loosen my grip only slightly, not letting her go but giving her more air so she can speak. "He told me about his v-vision. He s-said she would be your end."

My goddamn brother and his stupid visions. Even if it were to come true, how could Seraphine be the cause of it?

I slam my fist through the wall beside Havoc's head. She recoils, fear glittering in her green eyes. Tightening my grip again, I lean in until there is only a breath between us. I feel the blood in her veins run cold. I don't care. I want her dead. That's impossible, though. Like me, she can't die.

I throw her to the side, her body hitting the floor with a loud thud. She coughs and gasps as she draws gulps of air into her starving lungs. My rage cools, turning into bone crushing despair.

I stand, frozen, staring blankly ahead as visions of the eons to come I will spend without my woman playing on a loop inside my head. I hear Havoc's breathing returning to normal as she shakily pulls herself to her feet. From the corner of my eye, I see her take a tentative step closer. I shake my head and she immediately stops her advance.

"Leave. Now." My words are as cold as I feel now. In all my years, I have never felt a chill like this. I doubt I will ever be warm again. Not without her.

I take a deep breath, straighten my tie again, and run my hands through my disheveled hair before turning to face Havoc. She has tears streaming down her cheeks. I don't care. She was right when she said now I can get back to what I do best.

"I can't kill you, Havoc. But what I can do is something worse than death. And if you are ever so much as on the same continent as I am again, I can promise you that the only words you ever utter again will be nothing but unanswered prayers to God for swift and merciful release from the Hell I will put you in. Now, get the fuck out."

Her entire body shakes as I can only imagine the images of what I can do to her fill her mind. She nods slowly, as if trying to hide her fear from me and failing. The air was charged with the chill of my threat. The air of superiority she normally wears is gone. I can smell the fear rolling off of her in waves.

Without a word, she turns meekly away and leaves, the door softly clicking closed behind her. A sharp contrast to Seraphine's exit. I stare at the door, scowling at it as if it has personally offended me. After a few minutes, I sigh and return to my desk. Opening my laptop, I am met with the image of Seraphine I had set as my background.

It's a grainy image I had taken from the security camera photoage the first night I watched her in the VIP room. She was sitting on one of the red leather couches, though in this picture, there was no color. I only knew it was red because that was the color I had chosen for all of the private rooms. She is holding a glass of champagne, the delicate glass pressed against her perfect lips. I brush the tips of my fingers across the screen as a wave of emotion swells inside me. I tell myself it's for the best, but I would give up everything just to touch those lips one more time.

My sadness felt like a steel ball in my gut. I knew it was something I would carry with me until the end of all time. I close the laptop, unable to bear the sight for a moment longer. I rest my hands on top of the laptop, nauseated by the anguish I was feeling. Then, I do something I have never done in all my long life.

I cry.

CHAPTER

TWENTY-ONE

SAMUEL

Six Months Later

Part of me had hoped the next night when I walked into the club, Seraphine would be there waiting on me. The moment I stepped inside, though, I knew she was not there. I felt her absence in the air. It was the same feeling I have felt every day since she left.

Ricky had called me that day as well. He told me Seraphine had come home the night she found me with Havoc, packed a bag, and left. He said he made sure she made it to the bus station safely, but she refused to tell him where he was going. I thanked him for taking care of her and disconnected the call. When I stopped by her apartment a few days later, I fully expected him to attempt to fight me. He didn't though. He simply nodded at me when I stepped out of the car, then disappeared back inside the abandoned house he called home.

Walking into her apartment again was surreal. Almost everything was the same, but entirely different at the same time. Most of her things were still where they should be. The thin blanket she slept with every night was neatly folded on the bed. The tattered curtains were still hung over the cloudy windows. The soap and shampoo was still in the shower. Everything was as it always was. The only thing missing was her.

As I was leaving, I noticed the paintings still sitting in the corner of the room. I gathered them up and loaded them in the trunk of the car. Now they hang in my bedroom, a silent reminder of the woman I will never forget. I wake up every morning and stare at them, especially the self portrait of the night Sister Margaret saved her life.

I couldn't bring myself to return to the shelter. Eve still volunteered there regularly and kept me informed of anything that required my attention. I had ensured the shelter was well funded, but I still covered every utility bill and repair expense each and every month without fail. I'm certain Sister Margaret knew where the money was coming from, but she thankfully stayed away. I don't think I would be able to bear seeing her kind and knowing eyes again.

I never changed the background photo on my laptop. It was the only photo I had left of her. Each night, I would stare for hours at the image before I was able to start any semblance of work. Which is what I am doing when I hear the faint rapping on my office door. My shoulders slump at the sound. No one comes up here anymore. They have all learned to keep their distance from the sad sack that runs this place. Eve has been handling all of the stuff on the floor for months now. I am nothing more than a shadow taking up space in this building. Even Drakin keeps our interactions as brief as possible.

"Come in," I finally say after I take a moment to compose myself.

Eve tentatively peeks around the corner as she cracks open the door. When she is sure it's safe to enter, she takes a step inside and gently closes the door behind her. She twisted the ring on her finger nervously, looking anywhere but directly at me. Her deep brown eyes shimmered with the uneasiness she was obviously feeling.

I leaned back in my chair, crossing my arms over my broad chest as she cleared her throat. She opened her mouth a few times to speak, but no words would come out. I glared at her, frowning and wishing she would just spit it out already so I could get on with wallowing in my misery in peace.

"Just spit it out already, Eve," I huff, my annoyance with her inability to speak growing.

"I-I just," she stammered. She paused, closing her eyes as she took a deep inhale and blew it out slowly to calm herself. "I wanted to check on you. Everyone is concerned. *I* am concerned."

My lips thinned in irritation. Not at her, but at myself. I was pissed at the person I had become. No longer was I someone who struck fear into the hearts of all mankind. Now, I was someone to be *concerned* about. This would not do.

"I'm fine," I snapped at her, grabbing my phone off of the desk and shooting a quick text to Drakin.

ME

WE ARE LEAVING. TONIGHT.

I place the phone back down. I don't expect a reply until he has arranged a plane to take us back east. I can't stay here any longer, living like a ghost in this place. I have to get out so that I can suffer in silence without prying eyes looking at me like I am some kind of injured puppy in need of rescue.

"We both know you aren't," Eve says, her hands on her hips in the way a mother does when scolding a child they have caught in a lie.

I roll my eyes at her, closing my laptop and packing it away. My phone buzzes on the desk. I grab it and read the response Drakin has sent.

DRAKIN

New York, I assume.

DRAKIN

Yes.

DRAKIN

Who told you?

ME

Told me what?

I felt my pulse quickening inside me. What was I supposed to know that I didn't? My foot tapped rapidly under the desk as I waited for his next reply.

"You're leaving?" Eve asked, bringing my thoughts back to this room with her.

"Yes," I answer, frozen in a sort of limbo as I waited for

the next text. "I'm going back east. I'll send for you when I am resettled. Two weeks, tops."

Apprehension flickered across her beautiful face. She opened her mouth again to speak, but this time I waved her off before she could tell me what I now understood. She would not be coming with me this time. Eve had finally found her purpose. She was going to stay.

"I'll make sure you stay updated on Eden and the shelter," she nods. Then, without another word, she silently disappears through the door.

Once again, I am left alone with my scattered thoughts. The sound of the clock on the wall taunts me as the second hand ticks away, each tick sounding like a grenade exploding in the silence. What does he know that I don't? And what does it have to do with New York?

A million different scenarios play out in my mind. I've been so out of it the last six months, it could be anything. I have several businesses in New York, none of which I have been paying much attention to lately. Strip clubs, night clubs, even one live peep show, not to mention my penthouse where I used to call home. New York had been my home for the better part of the last decade before coming out here. Even if whatever I am missing isn't of any significance, it's time to go back where I belong.

The phone sits silently on my desk, mocking me. Every cell in my body vibrates with anticipation as I wait. It isn't until my chest starts to feel tight that I realize I have been holding my breath. After a few long minutes of silence, I return to my bag, grabbing a few other important documents from my desk and shoving them inside. I am so focused on getting the hell out of here now, when the phone finally does buzz again, I almost jump out of my skin.

The bag falls from my hands to the floor, some of the contents I had stuffed inside spilling out onto the carpet. My stomach tangled itself into a ball of angry knots, churning my insides to the point of discomfort. Before even looking at the incoming message, I can sense this is going to be something...unpleasant. The silence in the room grew tight with tension, almost strangling me as it wrapped itself around my throat. My hand shakes as I reach for the phone, half in anticipation, half in fear of what I was possibly about to learn. I pressed the button to unlock the device, and stared blankly at the screen as my brain tried to process the words on the screen.

DRAKIN

Travis has been located in New York.

All other emotions left me except for a blinding rage. All of the despair I had been feeling since Seraphine left, everything melted away and has left nothing but a fury I have not felt in a very long time.

The man who tortured my Seraphine, who kept her drugged up for days and passed her around like a communion cup until she was nothing but a broken, bloody mess, then dumped her in some back alley to die was finally within reach. I had actually all but forgotten I had charged Drakin with the task of tracking him down after the conversation with Sister Margaret in the garden all those months ago. I am just as furious now as I was when she first told me of the day she found Seraphine. If there were a Hell like the one described in the Christian Bible, he will be begging for me to send him there by the time I am finished with him.

I grab the phone and scoop up the bag from the floor, not bothering with the papers that fell out when I dropped it, and stomp towards the door. The wood cracks as I slam it closed behind me for the last time. I type out a quick text as I take the stairs two at a time, all but running out of the building.

ME

On my way to the airport. Have the plane ready when I get there.

I press the buttons on the screen with such force it cracks a little. As I hail a cab, not wanting to wait for Drakin to drive from the apartment to pick me up, I feel the phone buzz again in my palm.

DRAKIN

There's one more thing.

DRAKIN

I've gotten word he is stalking one of the girls at the peep show.

My rage morphs into something else. My stomach turns and my vision goes blood red. This is beyond anger. There isn't even a word in all the languages that are or ever have been to describe what I am feeling right now. Before the words even appear on the screen, I know what he is about to tell me.

DRAKIN

It's Seraphine.

CHAPTER

TWENTY-TWO

SERAPHINE

I'm not sure if I will ever get used to the noise of the city. Back in California, it was never this noisy. Sure, Ricky and his crew would play their music really loud, but that was different. This is traffic, screaming, sirens, and so many other sounds I still haven't been able to fully identify since I moved here. None of it sounds like music, and it's so constant. I feel like I can never hear myself think. Which is a blessing. I may hate all the noise, but at least it keeps my mind from drifting to thoughts of him.

Despite my best efforts, though, Samuel was never far from my mind. Images of him always seemed to pop up at the worst times. I've burned more meals than I can count over the last six months because I was lost in my memories. Memories of the nights we would spend together, the way his fingers felt against my skin, the things he would growl in my ear as he moved inside me, the arguments that always ended in sex, all of it. There wasn't a sound loud enough in the world to drown out those memories.

I rake my hand down my face as the alarm clock on the

nightstand beeps incessantly. Eight o'clock already. I feel like I haven't slept at all. Of course, I feel like that most every night since the night I left. Every time I close my eyes, all I see is the man I left behind.

I toss the blanket aside and begrudgingly swing my legs over the side of the bed. I feel like shit. All I want is to crawl back under the covers and let this soul crushing despair consume what is left of me. Unfortunately, my rent is due in a few days. So sinking into an even deeper depression is not an option.

If there is a silver lining in all of this, it's this apartment. It's not the most luxurious place in the world, but it is a considerable upgrade from the shithole I was living in back in Cali. There is even a full kitchen and an actual bathroom. Not a hint of particleboard in sight.

When Ricky dropped me off at the bus station, I checked my bank account at the ATM before buying my ticket here. I had been saving a good bit of money since Samuel was paying for most of my bills and I was no longer spending so much feeding everyone who was living at the empty lot. However, I knew there was no way I had saved a quarter million dollars in just a few weeks. No doubt the extra funds were deposited by Samuel. The sight of all those zeros only made the pain I was feeling worse.

I withdrew the few thousand I knew was actually mine and didn't touch another cent. I didn't want his guilt money. I would have closed the account, but I had no way to return the funds he had put there. The only thing I could do was let it sit there. If he had access to make the deposit, I was certain he had the ability to also see I wasn't spending any of it. Not even the interest the money had earned as it sat there in my account.

Luckily, when I stepped off the bus, I had enough to put a deposit on this place and buy a few essentials. The apartment came furnished with an actual bed, a sofa, a coffee table, and a couple of nightstands, so at least I didn't have to make any big purchases. A few dishes, some toiletries, a week's worth of groceries, and a few new outfits. I had left almost everything behind when I left. The few clothes I brought with me were just some of the older things I had never got around to moving into Samuel's apartment. I couldn't bring myself to go back to his place to get some of the newer things he had bought me.

It was early spring, but still bone chillingly cold out. I am always cold now. Pushing myself to my feet, I pad over to the closet and pull out some fleece lined leggings and an oversized sweater. When I get in the booth, it won't really matter what I put on now anyway. The money isn't as great as I made at Eden, but it's still pretty good. I don't have to worry about anyone trying to grab my ass while I dance, either. Three inch thick plexiglass has its advantages. I may be completely naked when I dance in the booths, but at least the lights keep me from being able to see whatever the men who come to watch are doing.

I pull my coat tighter around me as I step out of my building onto the sidewalk. The wind was especially bitter tonight. One drawback to working at the peep show booths was the hours. Sure, I worked nights at Eden also, but at least when I went in it was still light outside. The peep show, aptly named Babylon, didn't open until 10pm, though. Most of the time when I left at the end of my shift, the sun was just starting to peek over the tops of the buildings. It was usually the only sunlight I would see all day.

I scan the sea of faces, all on their way to somewhere I will never know, like I do every time I set foot outside. Part of me knows I am only torturing myself. In the six months since I left, he hasn't made any attempt to contact me. I tell myself it's for the best, but I thought he would at least make some kind of half-assed attempt to win me back. But he never did. Another part of me died a little more inside each day that passed and I didn't find him in this crowd of bustling strangers.

My face falls as I give up like I do every day and turn to walk the six blocks to Babylon. For a moment, I consider splurging on a cab, then quickly decide against it. It may be cold, but it's not that far of a walk. Also, if I take a cab, I won't get the chance to see if the art gallery has any new pieces in their window display. I haven't painted in months, but I keep telling myself I will get some new paints and canvases soon. Maybe one day I will, then I can see my own work on display in the window of the gallery.

The thought of painting reminds me I had to leave the three paintings I had in my old apartment behind. Not like I could have brought them with me. I have no idea what happened to those paintings. Most likely, Rita threw them out and they are now rotting in some landfill somewhere.

Pausing in front of the window, I take a moment to admire the new painting on display. The grays, reds, and black swirl together in a seemingly random way. To me, however, they remind me of the way Samuel's eyes would get an almost flaming glow to them when he was angry. I stand there, hypnotized by the painting and lost once again in my memories. I stare so long, my eyes start to lose focus, making the image seem more like the familiar set of eyes I would never see again.

A cab honks loudly and someone lets loose a stream of curses that would make a sailor blush, startling me back into the present. In the reflection of the glass window, I watch everyone moving around me. Most everyone seems so happy, except for the cursing man and the cabby, who are now in an all-out screaming match in the middle of the street. Neon light and traffic signals flash and blink all around me, bathing the world in their glow. I, however, am forever in the shadows no matter where I stand.

I let out a resigned sigh and check my watch. As much as I want to stay here and dream of my own work hanging in this very window someday, if I don't get a move on I will be late for work. Tim, the manager of Babylon, isn't overly strict, but he does expect all the girls to be ready and in their individual booths when the doors open.

Taking one final look at the painting, something in the reflection of the glass catches my eye. A face that seems familiar, though I can't immediately remember where I have seen it before. Squinting my eyes, I lean closer to the glass, not wanting to turn around to look at the man who seems to be watching me from across the street in case I am mistaken. I haven't exactly met anyone I would consider a friend since I moved to New York, but I swear I have seen this person before.

Bile rises in my throat as realization hits me like a sucker punch to the face. I spin around on my heel, but the man is gone. A million questions flood my brain, twisting and tangling until I feel like I am going to pass out. I sprint across the street, narrowly missing getting hit by a passing motorcycle, but he's gone by the time I make it to the opposite sidewalk. Was it really him? How did he even find me? It feels like an eternity since I last saw him. I wish it had been.

Every instinct is telling me to run back to my building, lock myself away in my apartment, pack my things, and leave on the next bus out of here. Thankfully, my logical side kicks in and I realize going home right now wouldn't be the safest option. If it were him, he could potentially follow me back to my place and I would have no one around to protect me. I hurry up the street, glancing over my shoulder every few seconds expecting to see him somewhere in the crowd behind me. If I can make it to Babylon, at least I will have witnesses if he tries anything.

When I am half a block away, I make the stupid decision to go in the back entrance so he doesn't see which building I go into if he really is following me somehow. There's a well-lit alley beside the building leading to the dumpsters of all the buildings on this block. The backdoor is hidden and there would be no way he would see me unless he already knows where it is.

I turn off the main sidewalk down the alley, breathing a sigh of relief when the door is in my sights only a few feet in front of me. My relief is short lived, though, as the backdoor swings open. My view is partially obstructed by the dumpster, and all I see is the top of the dark green metal door open then close again with a loud clank. Someone reaches up with a long steel pipe, shattering the light hanging above the door. The shards of glass sound like thousands of tiny bells as they scatter onto the pavement. A wave of panic like I have never felt overtakes my entire body, rooting my feet to the ground beneath me.

In my paralyzing fear, the world around me goes deafeningly quiet. I hold my breath, waiting for him to step closer so I can see his face again with my own eyes. Everything inside me twisted in an icy fear at what I was certain was about to be my final moments in this life. I've never been the praying type, despite Sister Margaret's best efforts, but right now I was whispering every prayer I ever knew and hoping there was someone out there listening.

Travis' barking laugh was bone chillingly terrifying. I covered my mouth to keep myself from screaming, naively thinking if he couldn't hear me, then he also couldn't see me. His footsteps as he stepped out from behind the dumpster echoed off the brick walls that surrounded us on either side. With the light shattered, I couldn't make out the details of his face, but I knew it was him.

He dragged the pipe along the pavement as he slowly walked forward, the sound like metal nails on a concrete board. Glancing over my shoulder towards the busy sidewalk behind me, I debated making a run for it. It was only twenty-five feet away. Thirty at the most. If I screamed loud enough, maybe someone would hear me and I would be safe. Looking back at him, though, we both knew I wouldn't make it two steps before he caught me. Despite his agonizing slow progression forward as he stalked closer to me, Travis was fast when he wanted to be. I didn't stand a snowball's chance in Hell of making it out of this alley safely.

A warm sensation ran down my legs as the piss soaked

my leggings. Travis stood over me, watching the puddle as it formed at my feet. He was so close I could smell the stench of his breath. I flinched, my body shaking violently as he reached forward and ran his index finger along my jawline.

"Don't for one second think a little bit of piss is going to stop me from what I am about to do to you, Seraphine." His voice was laced with the sick pleasure he was getting from this.

I could feel the vomit burning my throat, threatening to erupt at any moment. In the very depths of my being, I knew this time there would be no one to save me from this alley he is going to leave my broken body in. "H-How d-d-did you f-find me?" I stutter. I knew he had fled Cali last year after he stole a bunch of drugs from his supplier, but I had no idea he was living in New York. Even if I had known, this city is massive. The chances of him randomly spotting me on the street on the rare occasion I leave my apartment were still slim to none.

"One of the girls here is a customer," he smiles, leaning in to whisper his next words in my ear. "She sold you out for a few rocks and a dime bag."

A strangled sob rips through my body as I start to crumple to the ground. Travis catches me before I hit the concrete, pulling me against his chest as if he is comforting a lover. "Shhhh, little angel. Don't cry. Let me give you something to take all the pain away." He reaches into the pocket of his coat and pulls out a handful of mixed pills.

I push with every ounce of strength left in my weak body while he tries to force the pills into my mouth. He wraps my ponytail in his fist, yanking my hair in order to angle my head so he has better access. My scalp burns with pain, but I continue to blindly push and claw at whatever piece of him I can get my hands on. By some miracle, I land a single punch square on his nose. He groans as he stumbles backward a few steps. The pipe clatters to the ground as his grip on my hair loosens enough for me to break free.

Still dazed,I fall backwards without his grasp holding me up. My head connects with the pavement hard, knocking the wind out of my lungs in a rush. Everything around me goes blurry as I struggle to remain conscious. My ears are ringing, but I hear the sound of the metal door slamming against the side of the dumpster. I clamp my hands over my ears as the sound of some kind of unrecognizable beast roaring overwhelms my sensitive ears. A dark shadow blankets the alley. For a moment, everything is black.

"What the fuck?" Travis says in shock of whoever or *what*ever has come through the door.

I push myself upright just enough to see him grab the pipe again and raise it above his head. Everything is still spinning around me, but I am able to make out the faint outline of Travis as he taunts this thing. He swings wildly, which only seems to make it angrier. Rubbing my head, I watch in disbelief at the scene playing out in front of me.

The thing has to be at least seven feet tall, if not more. Huge black wings stretch the entire width of the alley. Each wing has a single black claw at its tip. They don't seem to be fluttering as if the thing is flying, but rather slashing at him like knives. Two massive red horns stick out from either side of the creature's head, a halo of fire and what appears to be barbed wire encircling them.

Travis swings the pipe again, but this time the creature

catches the pipe, along with his hand around the metal weapon, in its impossibly large fist. Travis pulls with all his might, trying to get out of the monster's grip, but the creature lifts him off the ground by the pipe as if he weighs nothing at all. The creature snarls and growls, white foam dripping from its mouth like a rabid beast. The smell of piss and shit assaults my nostrils as Travis sobs and screams like the scared little bitch he is.

The monster barks a booming laugh, grabbing Travis' free arm with its other hand. Its wings lower to its sides, allowing more moonlight to shine down into the dark alley. It's not enough to be able to see the creature clearly, but I can see its silhouette as he raises Travis higher. Rubbing my eyes, I struggle to process what I think I am seeing.

His eyes are glowing bright red, as are the cracks across his tan skin. Heat radiates from his body, cutting through the cold air like a knife. The warmth is as hot as fires from the very depths of Hell. Something about this comparison clicks inside my frazzled mind. Something Samuel said to me the last time I saw him.

"Because I am the Devil, Seraphine."

Holy. Fuck. It's him. This monstrous figure standing over me in this dark alley on a cold April night in New York City is the man I fell in love with. For whatever reason, probably shock, the only thought in my head is *I fucked the goddamn Devil.*

Travis begs incoherently for his life as he continues to sob. Samuel's eyes meet mine, completely ignoring the man whose life he literally holds in his hands. My vision is still a little blurred and my head spins out of control. Everything feels like it is moving in slow motion, like I am trapped inside a nightmare I can't wake up from. Suddenly, everything becomes too much for me to take. Turning my head to the side, I vomit violently everywhere.

When the contents of my stomach are thoroughly emptied on the ground beside me, I look back to Samuel, who is still holding Travis at least three feet off the ground by his arms. His expression was clouded with an anger I had never seen before. For a moment, I worried when he was finished with whatever he was planning to do with Travis, he would turn that anger towards me.

A fresh wave of nausea swept through me, and I gagged at the thought of what might happen. The feeling passed as quickly as it came on, though, as I looked into Samuel's eyes and saw more than just the unbridled rage behind the flames that danced in their fiery glow. For a fraction of a second, I saw the pain and sadness he was feeling at the sight of me on this cold pavement and knowing he was almost too late to save me. The moment passes in the blink of an eye, then it is gone. In its place is nothing but hatred as he turns his attention back to the man who was intent on killing me tonight.

The sound of Samuel's roar rips through the sound of the busy street only a few feet away. I am certain the sound can be heard for miles. Not even Travis' answering scream can be heard.

Samuel's skin stretches and cracks further than humanly possible, exposing more of the fire burning below his flesh. With his mouth open wide, I can see his normal pearl white teeth are replaced with multiple rows of razor sharp fangs. His long, slender forked tongue slithers out, wrapping around Travis' throat like a python squeezing its prey before eating it. Samuel's black wings expand again, encasing Travis as the claws rip into the flesh of his back.

The sound of Travis' screams fade into a wet gurgle as Samuel's tongue tightens around his throat. Crimson blood drips from the feathers of Samuel's wings, pooling on the pavement at his bare feet. It's not until now I realize Samuel is completely naked as the claws retract and pull chunks of meat from Travis' weakening body. His already large cock is even bigger in this unholy form of his body. It was already a bit of a struggle for him to fit inside me when we fucked. I can't imagine he would ever be able to fit that thing in my pussy.

Samuel's eyes are engulfed with the flames of his rage. His biceps bulge as he begins pulling Travis' arms in opposite directions. The sound of his flesh ripping away from the rest of his body makes a sickening sound. His bones crack as they break under Samuel's hands. A second or two later, his arms tear away from his torso, leaving him dangling in the air by Samuel's tongue still wrapped around his throat. Another moment later, Travis' face starts to swell and his eyes bulge from their sockets. They explode from his skull, spraying white clumps of glue all over Samuel's face. If I had anything left in my stomach, it would definitely be coming up right now.

I suddenly feel lightheaded, the edges of my vision closing in around me. Everything around me spins wildly out of control. The last thing I see before I lose consciousness is Travis' dead body hitting the ground. Samuel's wings and body start to shrink to a more recognizable size, the black wings folding around his arms and disappearing again into the tattoos that cover his arms.

I feel his hands slip underneath my limp body and lift me off of the cold concrete. His skin is still warm, the fiery crack in his skin having closed and knitted themself back together.

"I've got you, woman." His voice sounds muted and far away as he cradles me against his bare chest. Intangible words fall loosely from my cracked lips as the impending darkness takes me over.

Then, nothing.

TWENTY-THREE

SERAPHINE

The room is warm. This is the only coherent thought able to form in my brain as I feel the dream-like fog begin to lift. My next thought is *OW!* I groan in agony as my head feels like it has been split open in several places. I lift my heavy arms to rub my temples, but even this small action is torture.

I attempt to sit up, immediately regretting the decision. Pushing myself up on the incredibly soft mattress that is in no way mine, a sudden wave of nausea rolls in my stomach. This, along with the throbbing pain in my head, confirms I most definitely have a concussion. I hesitate to open my eyes, unsure if the light I am unsure is on or not in this unfamiliar room, will help me or only add to this pain.

I slowly and cautiously open my eyes. The first thing I see is the roaring fire in the fireplace of this very large, opulent bedroom. I scan the room and wonder how in the fuck I ended up here. The last thing I remember before passing out is standing on the sidewalk in front of the art gallery a couple of blocks from my apartment.

I recall the painting with its black and red coloring swirled together on the canvas. There was something else, though. Something on the edge of the haze still clouding my mind I couldn't quite make out. Closing my eyes again, I try to push myself through the fog of my memories. I watch myself leaning forward, staring at something on the glass. What was I looking at so closely?

I focus on the painting, assuming I must have seen something in the swirling colors that caused me to pass out. Suddenly, another fragment of the puzzle clicks into place. I wasn't looking at the painting. I was looking at the reflection in the glass.

All the events of the previous night come rushing back to me in a flood of memories. Travis, the alley, pissing myself in terror, large black wings, and so much blood. I am instantly wide awake, remembering who it was that saved me from certain death.

Samuel.

My eyes fly open, searching anxiously around the room for a way to escape before he realizes I am awake. There are only two doors in the room, one of which is open, leading into what I assume is the bathroom. I have no idea what lies waiting for me on the other side of the only other door. Even if he isn't out there, there is no way I would be able to make it out of wherever the hell I am without him catching me.

I fling the covers off my body, almost falling out of bed as I rush over to the row of curtains covering what I pray are unlocked windows. Maybe, if I'm not too high up, I can at least jump down to make my escape. I tear open the heavy crimson velvet curtains, expecting to be met with bright sunlight. I preemptively shield my eyes. It takes me a second to realize there is no sunlight. All of the windows are covered in near-black tint. I can't tell if the sun is even shining outside. Everything is covered in darkness. The one thing I can make out is thick iron bars on the other side of the glass.

A cold knot twists and tightens in the pit of my stomach when I hear the doorknob turning. I consider trying to bolt into the bathroom. If I can lock myself inside, maybe I can find some other way out. Remembering what I saw last night, I know locking myself in the bathroom will be about as effective as taking on a tank with a piece of tissue paper. Samuel could rip the doors off the hinges without even breaking a sweat. Then, he would tear me apart the same way he did to Travis.

My heart thunders erratically inside my chest. The door creaks as it slowly swings open. Samuel takes a cautious step inside, closing the door carefully behind him, as if he is approaching a cornered animal and trying to judge how it will react to his presence.

A tense silence stretches between the two of us, engulfing the air and making it feel heavy. To my complete surprise, he looks as if he has always looked to me. His eyes are the same deep brown color. His raven black hair is still damp from a recent shower. The fine material of his crisp white shirt and dark blue slacks hug his muscles the exact way I remember they did the last time I saw him in California. Everything about him is the same, yet entirely different all at once.

Samuel shifts his weight from one foot to the other nervously. He looks down at his shoes, then back up to me a few times. He can't seem to keep his eyes on me for more than a few seconds at a time, though. The veins running along the side of his neck are tense and I can see the muscles in his face twitch. He is clenching his jaw tight, like he is struggling to remain in control of some raw emotion. Seeing him like this, acting more human than I can ever recall him being, strangely puts me a little bit at ease.

"Hi," is the only word I can manage to force out without completely breaking down.

"Hello, Seraphine." His voice is husky and hoarse, but the sound of my name on his lips after all this time is more than I can bear.

I crumple to the ground as the steel weight of everything I had been through comes crashing down around me. Earth shattering sobs racked my body. I didn't have the strength to hold it all back any longer, so I let everything I was feeling take over. Hot tears burned my skin as I cried harder than I have ever cried before.

Even with the fire still burning, my body was so cold it was almost numb. I didn't even realize how cold I was until I felt Samuel's warmth against my skin. He gently wrapped his arms around my trembling body and helped me to my feet. Gathering me in his arms, he cradled me the same way he did last night as he carried me back over to the bed.

I didn't expect him to lay down beside me, but that is exactly what he does. Toeing off his shoes, he pulls the soft blanket around the both of us. He pulls me onto his chest, hugging me tightly to him like nothing bad had ever happened between us. But it had. He had cheated. I had left. And he was the Devil he always told me he was.

"I never touched her," he says, breaking the silence

as if he has just read my mind. "I never touched anyone after the first time I met you on that abandoned lot."

I prop my chin on his chest to look up at the face I have dreamed of every night for the past six months. Samuel's unfocused eyes stare blankly ahead at the flames as they dance across the logs. His Adam's apple bobs up and down as he swallows hard.

"I didn't know she was going to be there. Not until I walked into the club with you. But I felt her presence as soon as I stepped inside."

"Sensed her?" I ask, still trying to come to terms with who and what he is.

He nodded once, his eyes still watching the fire. "Most of the time, we can sense each other," he explains.

"Sa-" I stop myself before saying his name. I'm unsure what to call him now. "Who is she?"

"She goes by Havoc. Your kind knows her as Lilith."

I take a deep breath as the reality finally starts to set in. My head spins with a million questions. Only one, though, is clear enough for me to ask it.

"Why?"

"Why, what?"

"Why didn't you tell me?"

The corner of his mouth twitches up a fraction of an inch as he turns his tearfilled eyes to mine. "Would you have believed me, woman?" he huffs.

"Probably not," I chuckle softly.

He presses a tender kiss to my forehead, his lips lingering against my skin. I feel his tears as they slip from his eyes. I guess the Devil has a heart after all.

"I don't even know what to call you," I whisper as I lay my cheek back against his chest.

My words apparently amuse him. His chest vibrates with his laughter. "Names are a human construct. One of the few things you people came up with I actually liked. When you've lived as many lives as I have, though, names lose all their meaning. You can call me anything you like, as long as you call me yours."

All of the broken pieces of my heart somehow find their way back to each other inside my chest with his words. I squeeze my arms around him, terrified if I ever let him go again he will disappear into the darkness. He winces in pain, trying to hide the way his face screws up as he groans. I will admit, the fact I just made the Devil himself feel even an ounce of pain does bring me more than a little bit of joy.

"You don't have to look so pleased with yourself," he chuckles softly. "This is your fault in more ways than one."

"How is it my fault?" I laugh, tracing the outline of one of the buttons on his shirt.

"I never felt pain before..." his voice trails off, fading away with words he didn't want to say.

"Before when?"

"Before you left." His words held a deep sadness within them. "For as long as I can remember, which would be longer than you could possibly comprehend, I was numb. Not just to pain, but to everything. The night you left, though, it was like something inside me broke. Or maybe it was fixed. I don't know, but what I *do* know is, since you left I have done nothing but feel."

"Ho-how old are you, Samuel?" I ask, already half knowing what he is going to say.

"There is no measure of time to explain how long I have been in existence. Not as old as God, but older than some other deities. I'm not sure how to explain it. According to the government, though," he laughs, "I am the tender young age of forty."

"Samuel?" The question I have next for him is the one I am most afraid to ask.

"Hmm?"

"Do I still have a soul? After everything we have...*done* together, everything you have done *for me*, did I make a deal I can never escape from?"

His warm fingers brush the hair that has fallen away from my face. Titling my chin up, he presses a chaste kiss to my cold lips, warming them with his own. "You will always have your soul." He tilts his head to the side slightly, his eyes getting a mischievous look in them. "Your previous landlady, however, is another story."

"Well," I huff. "That explains a few things. Anyone else?"

"From your life? Not that I am aware of. In general? Yes. Many, many, *many* more."

"How?"

"How do I find them or how do I take their souls?"

"Both, I guess."

"For the most part, they find me," he explains. "I don't actually seek out anyone with the intent of making a deal with them. Not in a long time, anyway. When I did, it was usually for a good reason. Well, good to me anyway."

"What reason could be considered good enough to steal someone's immortal soul?" For some reason, his answer made me angry.

"Bragging rights," he says with a shrug, like that was all the reason he needed to do what he did to those people. "The ultimate fuck you to God." The corners of his mouth twitch upwards again, pleased with the reminder of how many souls he has prevented over the years from entering Heaven.

I never was much of a religious person growing up. On the rare occasion my mother would attempt to get clean, she would take me with her to one church or another for a Sunday or two, so I know the basics about God and the Bible. One thing I do remember from recall from those random Sunday school lessons is the story of Lucifer and why he was kicked out of Heaven for rebelling. He hated humans so much, he led a revolt against the other angels and lost.

"You hate us," I whisper, more to myself than to him.

"I do." Those two little words slice into me like a knife. The feel of his thumb stroking my cheek is like sandpaper against my skin. "I hate them all. But I could never hate you."

"Why?" I ask with a crack in my voice.

His lips press into a thin line, but he doesn't elaborate further. "The how is a little easier to explain. At its core, your soul is energy. When a deal is made, the energy is transferred as payment. I give you what it is you want most in this life, you give me your soul. The agreement between us is binding, and neither of us can break it without consequences."

"I can't imagine wanting anything so badly I would be willing to burn for eternity to get it." I shudder at the thought of spending my afterlife in suffering for a few years of leisure here on Earth.

"Desperate people do desperate things," he explains. "And your storytellers got a lot wrong when they decided to write that book. Heaven, Hell, Limbo. None of those places really exist."

I suddenly feel very sad at the knowledge there is nothing waiting for me on the other side of this life when I die. All my life, the one thing that got me through the dark times was the belief I would finally have peace at the end of it all. Hearing there would be nothing but darkness is disheartening to say the least, but also raises another question.

"If Hell isn't real, what happens to the souls you...collect?"

"I keep them inside me, so to speak. When the person dies, their soul is not permitted to fully rest. The best way I can explain it is that it's a lot like having insomnia. You would feel exhausted, but never allowed to sleep. There isn't exactly any pain, but there is no relief either."

"What about everyone else?"

He shrugs again. "Euphoria."

Samuel pulls my lips to his again, this time trailing feather-light kisses along the line of my jaw. "Can we talk about this another time?"

My brain fuzzes and my eyes flutter closed. Part of me demands more answers from him, but another part has other ideas entirely. It had been so long since anyone had touched me. Despite all of the revelations of the past 24 hours, my body ached for him. Without me even realizing it, Samuel had somehow unlocked a part of me I had kept hidden away for so very long. Here, in arms of the Devil, I felt more alive than ever.

My fingers fumbled with the buttons of his shirt. A desperate need to feel his skin against mine took over me. Samuel's chest vibrated with a low growl as his lips found mine again. We clawed at each other almost violently in our need. The growing heat of his body flowed deliciously into mine, spreading to every nerve and setting them each on fire.

"You are mine, woman," he whispered, his hot breath tickling my neck as he stamped kisses along the side of my throat.

"Forever?" I ask in a breathless moan, my nails digging into his back as I slid his shirt off his shoulders.

"Forfuckingever."

Samuel's arms wrapped themself around my body, flipping me onto my back without breaking our contact. He straddled my hips, sitting back on his knees as he tore at the gold buckle of his belt. He hastily kicked his slacks and the blanket covering us to the floor. The bulge in his briefs made my mouth water as he gazed down in appreciative appraisal of my body.

Following his eyes, I realize I am dressed only in an oversized white shirt and a pair of new cotton panties. I was so focused earlier on escaping, I didn't notice I was half naked. My skin tingles at the rush of cool air, sending a shiver of anticipation down my spine at the thought of things to come.

Samuel braced his hands on either side of my body, leaning down over me with a lustful hunger in his eyes. The air around us was charged with energy. His lips brushed softly against mine before moving lower to caress the hollow dip of my clavicle. A long, anguished moan escapes from somewhere deep inside me. My back arches off the bed and my fingers grip the sheets for dear life.

Samuel's lips rediscover me slowly. His warm tongue traces a line across my collarbone, then up the side of my throat. I feel his fingers grip the material of my shirt, pulling it taut until the fabric starts to tear away from my body. I press my lips to the lines of the wing tattoo across his shoulder, his flesh growing warmer as I run my fingers along the intricate lines. One of the feathers separates from his flesh and tickles my skin.

His body swelled under my hands, his mouth devouring me with an increasing hunger. Images of the night before invade my mind. The way he looked so monstrous terrified me. Now, though, the thought of him reclaiming me like that excites me.

Samuel grinds his erection against my throbbing pussy. My nipples harden into diamond hard peaks against his chest. His hand sear my skin a path across my burning skin as he rakes his fingers up my thigh, hooking my leg and wrapping it around his waist. Moving higher, he hooks his thumb under the fabric of my panties, ripping them away without any effort at all.

"I have missed your taste on my tongue," he whispers against my skin as his head dips lower.

A sharp pain rushes through my body. My eyes fly open to meet his burning gaze. Flames dance in the darkness of his irises. A sinister smile twists across his face, revealing the rows of sharp teeth he drags across my flesh.

The fork of his devilish tongue laps at the fresh tiny

punctures dotting my inner thigh. My head falls back against the pillow as the pain melts away under his touch. I moan loudly when he repeats the processes on the opposite leg, licking away the drops of blood as they run down my leg.

I am shocked at how my body responds to him in this form. There had always been something about him that called to a place inside me I didn't know existed, but this was different. He is, after all, the fucking Devil. I should be terrified as his black wings rise from the lines of his tattoos covering his arms, shoulders, and back. Instead, explosive currents of electricity course through my veins.

A hot ache grows in my cunt when I feel his snakelike tongue slither between the dripping wet flesh between my thighs. "Oh, God, yes!" I cry out between strangled gasps for air.

Samuel hisses his displeasure at my choice of words. His tongue lashes at my clit like a whip. I groan in half pain, half pleasure at the sensation.

"God is not here, woman," he grits out between the blades of his teeth. "Only me."

The claws of his massive wings dig into the mattress, replacing his hands to hold him up. With one hand, he spreads my open wider so he can continue his assault on my pussy with his tongue. The other hand slides up my body and cups my breast. He twists and plucks at my nipple, his fingers working in unison with his tongue to bring me to the edge of oblivion.

"The fruit of the forbidden tree didn't taste as sweet as your cunt."

"Samuel," I breathe. "Please."

He chuckles as he sucks at my aching clit. "An entire choir of angels singing will never compare to the sound of you begging me for your release. Do you wish to come, woman?"

"Yesssss!"

"Not until I have had my fill of you." His words held an unspoken command. Do not come. "You asked me what Heaven is like, but I intend on showing you that Hell is where you belong."

I growl out my frustration, digging my nails into whatever skin of his I can. I fight to remain in control of my body. The need to come is almost overwhelming, but I somehow manage to keep it under control.

Cracks start forming across his tan skin. Tiny orange flames dance across his body, but somehow do not burn me. Large horns emerge on either side of his head, and a fiery halo of barbed wire twists around them. His entire body has shifted from the Samuel I know to the Devil I love.

The word catches in my throat before it can escape from my lips. I always thought love was for other people. It was some unattainable dream to me. I was a reformed druggie stripper from a broken family who used to sell her body for the heroine she shot into her veins. Love was not a word I had ever heard, nor was it something I had ever felt. Here, now, though, with his head between my legs as he worshiped my pussy with his forked tongue, I am consumed with it.

"I could eat your cunt forever and never get my fill," he says as he pulls his head from between my thighs. He places a tender kiss to each of the bites he marked me with earlier before crawling up the length of my body. The heat of his skin wraps around me like a security blanket. As long as I am in his arms, I know I am safe from the evils of the world.

He covered my mouth with his, his tongue plunging in and exploring the recesses of my mouth. This was not a chaste kiss by any means. This was a reclaiming of what was once lost and found again. The breath in my lungs was not stolen by him as he continued to claim my lips with his. I gave it to him freely of my own will.

I'm not sure if his briefs tore away as he transformed, or if they melted against the flames on his skin. Either way, his cock was no longer restrained by the fabric. It moved between us against my skin as he rocked his hips forward.

His cock felt so much bigger than it had before. I remember seeing it last night, thinking there was no possible way it could fit inside me. Feeling it bump against my entrance now sent a jolt of fear throughout my body. Taking him before had always been a bit of a struggle. This would be impossible.

Samuel's lips moved along my jaw and down my throat. One hand hooked my leg behind the knee, pulling my open as far as the laws of physics would allow. The solid length of his cock slid between the lips of my pussy as he slicked himself with my juices.

"You can take it, Seraphine," he whispers against my skin.

"I can't," I protest.

"Yes, you fucking can." He pushed himself into me slightly, already stretching and filling me more than anyone ever had before.

"No!" I cry out, fear gripping my throat like a vice. "It's too much. Too big."

He pushed himself in further, ignoring my protests. "You were made to take my cock, Seraphine. And that is *exactly* what you are going to do. Now be a good fucking girl, and take it!"

I scream as he forces himself deeper inside me. I tangle my fists in his hair, digging my nails into his scalp. His teeth sink into my shoulder, the pleasure mixing with the pain as I adjust to the feeling of him. A few moments later, my screams melt into moans. His teeth release my flesh as he slowly begins to move inside me.

"I knew you could take me," he praises, licking my wound clean. "You can take every inch I give you. Because you are fucking mine. Not God's. Not Heaven's. *Mine.*"

"Yes," I breathe against him, my hips matching his as he moves. "Yours."

If he didn't own my soul before, he did now. I didn't understand before how someone could give that part of themself over to him. I get it now. I would sell anything to him to feel him inside me forever. Never has anything in my life felt so good before.

Each thrust was harder than the last. Still, he moved with a torturously slow pace. I bucked my hips against him with an unsatiated need to come. Samuel's booming laughter at my attempts to make him fuck me faster shakes the walls of the room.

"Greedy cunt," he laughs. "You will get more when I fucking give it to you."

I growl in frustration as he presses me further into the mattress, pinning me in place so I can no longer move. He pulls his hips back, looking between us at his cock only just barely still inside me. His dick glistens in the light with my wetness. Lifting my chin with his thumb, his glowing eyes bore into mine.

"You are going to take everything. Because everything is exactly what I am going to give you." His words are a command not to be questioned.

Without waiting for my response, he slams himself forward into me. My back bows again, the sweetest pain I have ever felt tearing through every inch of my skin. There is no pause to allow for me to adjust this time. As soon as he bottoms out inside me, he pulls himself back and does it again. Over and over, he pounds me into a blissful oblivion from which I hope I never return.

"Take. It. Take. It. Take. It. Take! It!" Each word is punctuated with a thrust. Everything around us fades away as my senses are overwhelmed by desire. The sound of his skin slapping against mine echoes off the walls. My head spins wildly out of control as the edge of the cliff comes closer.

His lips covered mine again as his hands fondled the round globes of my breasts. He rolls my tiny, marble hard nipples between his thumb and forefinger. The combination of sensations pushes me closer to the edge. I don't know how much longer I can withstand this before I explode.

Samuel's body starts to tense. The corded muscles of his arms strain against his flesh. My body squirms beneath his as we both inch closer to the release we are chasing. Bright white dots cloud my vision as the end draws ever closer.

Samuel lets loose a deafening roar as he pours himself

into me, pumping everything he has to give into my starved body. I explode around as I am filled with the warmth of his cum. Together, we both explode into a million blazing hot pieces of starlight and brimstone. Pure ecstasy crash into me like waves of the ocean. The bed cracks beneath us as we ride out the final tremors of our climax.

It feels like an eternity passes before the ringing in my ears starts to subside. My heart slows to a more normal rhythm, and my breath returns to normal as I come down from my high. Samuel has made me come before, but never like this.

"You were holding yourself back before, weren't you?"

"A little," he chuckles softly, pressing a tender kiss to the tip of my nose.

The flames in his eyes die down, returning to the deep brown they once were. The cracks of his skin make a sizzling sound as they knit back together. The halo disappears, and the horns sink back into his skull. He pulls the claws of his wings out of the torn mattress, leaving two gaping holes in their wake. The feathers of his wings start to fall back in place along the lines of his tattoo. In another moment, he will be exactly as he was.

"Wait." I run my fingers along the silky edge of one of his feathers. "Can these stay? For just a while longer."

Samuel's expression softens, but he doesn't speak. The parts of his wings that had already reattached themself separate again from his flesh. He rolls to his side, wrapping us both in the inky darkness. The singular talons on each wing hook together as his arms hug me against his body, surrounding us both in the warmth of the words neither of us need to say.

TWENTY-FOUR

SAMUEL

f ever there were someone unworthy of forgiveness, it would be me. When I walked into this bedroom last night, I was prepared to receive the full force of her wrath before she walked out of my life again. What I didn't expect was her acceptance. For as long as I have been walking this earth, people have turned away from me in fear upon realizing who and what I am. In that alley, she saw the full extent of the darkness I so desperately tried to shield her from. And in this bed, she made love to it.

I stretch the stiffness of sleep out of my body as my wings fold back into place on my skin. Reaching out my arms to pull my woman closer, I find nothing but cold sheets. My eyes fly open as they scan the room for her. My first thought is she must be in the shower. But the door is open and there is no sound or movement to indicate this is the case.

I bolt upright, the air in the room several degrees colder than when we fell asleep, and rush to the door. I pull it open with enough force to rip it partially off its hinges.

Seraphine gasps in fright on the other side, spilling some of the hot coffee she is carrying on her hands.

I breathe out a momentary sigh of relief at the sight of her. She mumbles curses under her breath and pushes past me to set the two mugs she is carrying down on the small dressing table beside the fireplace. I push the door back into place enough to close it and pad across the plush carpet to assess the damage to her delicate skin.

I take her hand in mine, but she quickly pulls it away with another flurry of curses. I shoot her a look that tells her not to test me right now, and take her hand again. The skin is bright red, but no lasting damage seems to have been done. I chuckle softly, press a kiss to her cheek, and push her towards the bathroom to run some cold water on it.

"Had I known *this* would be my reward, I would have let you make your own damn coffee," she shouts from the bathroom, clearly annoyed.

"Had you stayed in bed like a good girl, your reward would have been something much different," I huff, grabbing my discarded slacks from the floor and slipping them back on.

She mumbles another slew of curse words under her breath as she reenters the bedroom, her scalded hand wrapped in a gray towel. I pick up the still steaming mugs, passing the one with more cream than actual coffee in it to her as I take a sip of the other. Begrudgingly, she takes it from my hand, letting out a soft moan when the warm liquid touches her lips. My eyes glance to the marks on her shoulder peeking out from under the collar of the white satin robe she is wearing, reminding me of her making the same sound as I moved inside her last night.

I feel myself hardening inside my pants at the memory. She did so well, not that I expected any less of her. My woman took everything I gave her, like I told her she would. My true form would have killed a lesser female. But not my Seraphine. She was made to take every inch.

Her skin breaks out in fresh goosebumps as she shivers and lowers herself into one of the wingback chairs next to the fireplace. There are still a few embers burning on one of the logs, but not nearly enough to heat the large bedroom. Setting my mug down, I grab a couple logs and a knotted bunch of kindling from the neatly stacked pile next to the fireplace. I arrange the wood just right, blowing on the embers to stoke the flames until they catch. It doesn't take long before the fire is roaring again. Seraphine holds her mug close to her face, smiling to herself and letting the warmth wash over her. I don't believe in perfect moments, but if I did, sitting here drinking coffee with her would be it.

"Samuel?" she asks, turning her big gray eyes to meet mine.

"Hmm?"

"Where the fuck are we?"

I chuckle softly at the wording of her question. "One of my properties."

"*One*?" Her brows shoot up almost to her silvery white hairline. "How many others are there?"

"More than this one," I smirk, beaming with egotistical pride.

She narrows her eyes at me before calling me, "Asshole."

"*Your* asshole," I correct, pressing a soft kiss to the tip of her nose. "I'm actually a bit surprised you were able to find the kitchen in this place. It's not in the same room as the shower, like I know you've grown accustomed to." I give her a wink. She gives me a death stare. Both of us laugh.

"I wouldn't be too surprised. It took me almost an hour of wandering up and down more hallways than I knew were architecturally possible to fit inside a single building 'til I did find it."

"Another reason I don't come here very often," I scoff, looking around the obscene opulence of the room. "While I like the seclusion of being in the middle of nowhere, it's far too big for me. When I had it constructed a little over a century ago, I used it more often. Now, it's become more of a hideaway than a home."

"Did you say you *built* this place? A *century* ago?" Her eyes are as wide as dinner plates. The cartoonish surprise on her face makes me laugh.

"Well, according to the paperwork, my great grandfather built it," I explain. "I only inherited it after his passing."

She shakes her head in disbelief, still trying to wrap her head around just how old I really am. "How long did it take you to find your way back here?" I laugh, stirring the fire with the wrought iron poker.I pick up another log and toss it on top to keep the flames from dying down too quickly. "Judging by the looks of your hand, you fared better on the return trip since the coffee was still hot enough to do that to you."

"Yeah," she chuckles, unwrapping her hand to examine it again. The redness has all but disappeared, and there's no sign of any swelling. She flexes her finger and winces slightly, though. I take her hand in mine again, this time to remove the pain she is feeling. "How the fuck did you just do that?" She asks in amazement, pulling her hand away and flexing her fingers again without any trouble.

"Perks of the position, I guess you could say," I tell her with a weak smile.

She pushes herself to her feet and up on her tiptoes, encircling her slender arms around my neck. "Any other...*perks* you care to tell me about?" Her eyes cloud with lust, becoming a stormy sea of her desire. I could drown in those eyes and die a happy man.

"You, lost in a clouded sea, as the life drained from your earthly body."

My brother's words echo inside my head. I don't know why I couldn't see it before. What Michael saw was not my physical death, but the death of something inside me. The life draining from my eyes wasn't my own, it was the death of everything I was before I met her. She is the storm and the raging sea. "Seraphine."

Her head tilts in confusion. She looks at me, her brows knitting together, trying to figure out why my demeanor has changed so suddenly. "What's wrong?"

"It's you," I whisper in horror.

"Samuel, you're scaring me," she says, her voice trembling, taking several steps backward away from me.

"He must have put the pieces together when Havoc told him about you," I continue, panic tightening in my chest. "He knew I would eventually find you. He could see everything, except this."

"Samuel!" Seraphine yells at me, fear and panic marring

the beautiful features of her face. "Tell me what the hell you are talking about!"

"He thinks you are going to be the death of me?" My voice is calm, despite the flurry of tangled thoughts swirling around in my head.

"What?" My response has no doubt raised more questions for her than it answered.

"He's coming." This realization hits me like a ton of bricks. One characteristic of angels is being able to feel the presence of one another when in close proximity. It's how he knew where I was when he came to see me in my office that day. It's how he knows where to find me now.

Michael must have heard from Havoc about Seraphine leaving that night. He knew I wouldn't be able to stay away from her forever. He had seen what he thought was my demise. He thought, even though she left, we would eventually find each other again. His visions are never wrong. But now I see, they are often misinterpreted.

"Samuel, I need you to tell me what the fuck is going on," Seraphine says, tears growing like storm clouds in her eyes. "Who is coming?"

"My brother," I say, already feeling him nearby. "Michael."

A flash of blinding white light fills the room before I have the chance to warn Seraphine to run. I hear her scream, the sound piercing my ears. My brother comes into focus, dressed in all white like the stereotypical fucker he is, holding a large steel sword embellished with golden flames on the hilt. His signature accessory to complete his ensemble. I hate myself now for not killing him all those millenia ago when I had the chance.

The blinding light from his grandiose entrance begins to fade. Michael stands in front of me, his righteous condemnation radiating from every cell of his being. He is within striking distance of Seraphine, but he is going to have to go through me first.

My brother's eyes move between Seraphine and myself. He is carefully sizing up the situation before he makes his move. I know he can sense he is going to have to kill me if he has any chance of killing her. In doing so, however, he will have done the very thing he is trying to prevent; my death.

"Hello, Michael," I say cautiously, trying to divert his attention long enough to figure out how I can get my woman out of here without her getting injured.

"Lucifer," he nods in response. He turns to Seraphine, who is crying on the floor as she hugs her knees to her chest for protection. "I am sorry we have to meet this way, Seraphine," he says to her without an ounce of remorse in his voice. "I hope you understand when I had the vision of my brother's death, I never imagined it was someone as lovely as you whom I would need to protect him from. I feel no pleasure for what I have to do."

"Bullshit," I scoff. "You said it once yourself, *dear brother*. You are the Flaming Sword of God. This is what you do. And I know for a goddamn fact you take a lot of pleasure from it."

He doesn't bother arguing with me. He knows I am not wrong. "When I was made aware of her existence, I planned on doing this much sooner. However, I was told my brother drove you away. I assumed in an effort to protect you from myself, but I soon learned that was not the case.

Have you told her why you thought it best to drive her away the way you did?"

"Doesn't matter why anymore, Michael." I spit the words at him vehemently. I know what he is playing at now. He not only means to kill her, he means to crush her soul entirely so that her rest in death will be plagued with sadness and pain.

"I take that as a no, then," he laughs. Turning back to Seraphine, he pins her with his stare. "Selflessness was never my brother's strong suit." He clicks his tongue as he shakes his head slowly. "I'm sure he told you the reason he pushed you away like he did was because he wanted to protect you from the monster he became after his failed coup. He probably even convinced himself that was the reason why."

"Quit stalling, Michael, and raise your fucking sword," I growl, feeling my skin heat with the rage building inside my chest.

He ignores me as he takes a step closer to Seraphine. I take a step closer to him, positioning myself fully between him and her. He stops his advance, but does not take his eyes off of hers. Seraphine has stopped crying, but is still sitting frozen in terror on the floor. I position myself in a defensive stance, preparing for whatever Michael may try to get to my woman.

"You are so beautiful, Seraphine," Michael continues, ignoring my presence entirely as he speaks directly to her. "More beautiful than even I could have ever imagined. I can see why my brother took a liking to you. However, your beauty will not stop the hands of time. You will grow old, and you will eventually die. It is an unfortunate truth about mortality. Eventually, your life will come to an end, while his life will go on until eternity's end."

"Shut up!" I scream, my booming words shaking the very foundation of the house.

"It was not your protection he was concerned with. It was his own. He has no desire to care for you in old age. He does not want to watch as your beauty fades and the light in your eyes slowly dims."

"Stop it!"

"He doesn't want mortality."

"Michael, stop!"

"He doesn't want you."

"Enough!"

Everything moves in slow motion. I feel my body propel itself forward as I lunge at my brother. However, it is more as if I am watching everything from outside my own body. Michael raises his sword over his head. I bear my razor sharp teeth at him. Both of our sets of wings explode off our skin. Seraphine screams, covering her face with her arms like a shield.

I reacted to his antagonizing too fast, too recklessly, and without a plausible plan of attack. My brother has the upper hand in more ways than one. While Michael still has the luxury of being emotionless, I allowed him to manipulate mine and coerce me to make the first move. The realization of this fatal mistake comes to me too late, though.

Everyone assumes because we are immortal, there is nothing that can kill us. Immortals, however, know differently. Angel can be killed. By one thing and one thing only. The sword my brother is currently bringing down over my head.

I expected my life to flash before my eyes at this moment. That's what people say happens right before you die. For me, though, I did not relive every moment in the eternity since my creation. Instead, all I could see was her. As I watched the blade that would put an end to the Devil himself draw nearer to its mark, visions of the life I could have had with Seraphine dance in front of my eyes. If I am destined to die here, I will fight until my last breath to ensure she gets to live.

Michael's sword is so close, I can feel the air as it slices into it. I close my eyes, seeing my beautiful woman, bracing for the impact. It feels as if an eternity passes, and still the blow does not come. I open my eyes again, expecting to see my brother still standing in front of me. What I see, however, I could never have imagined in a million lifetimes I would ever see again.

"Hello, my son."

TWENTY-FIVE

SAMUEL

I knew I recognized those eyes from somewhere. It had been a lifetime, though, since I had seen them. Several lifetimes, actually. Not since my expulsion from Paradise have I looked into the all-knowing irises of God. However, I never thought I would see those eyes staring back at me from the face of Sister Margaret.

Birds sing a sweet melody overhead. The trees sway in the warm breeze as it blows through their branches. Soft blades of green grass tickle the bottoms of my feet as the waves lap gently at the shore of a massive lake stretching for as far as my eyes can see. Heaven may not be a physical place like the Good Book would lead someone to believe, but the place where God presides is about as close to Heaven as anyone could hope for.

She stands without assistance, tall and proud, as you would expect a creator of worlds would. The deep lines of her face appear now to be less from a long and well lived life, and more from uncountable eons of wisdom. The putrid smell of the cancer that was eating away at her earthly form has been replaced with the familiar scent of lavender and sandalwood. This is the God I once loved more than anything.

I stand before my maker in absolute awe and admiration. All of the hatred I have harbored for so long melts away as tears prick my eyes. I never thought I would be forgiven for the atrocities I have committed. I know I do not deserve it. However, looking into the very eyes of God, I know it is all water under the proverbial bridge now.

"Why didn't you tell me?" I ask, choking back a sob of both joy and sadness.

"Would you have believed me if I had?" she laughs, using the same words I have said to Seraphine so many times before.

"No, probably not." We both stand and stare, a long silence stretching between us, for the longest of moments. "Why did you bring me here?" I ask, more than a bit confused.

She releases a heavy sigh, turning to look out over the peaceful water. "I felt it was time I intervened in what was happening."

"You mean with Michael."

She nods once. "Your brother has always had this misguided need to protect his brothers and sisters. I thought giving him the gift of foresight would help him to see threats more clearly, so that he may protect us all better. I know now, though, that was not the case."

"He is going to kill Seraphine because of these visions. You knew that was his plan. Why did it take you so long to step in?" The fear I feel for my woman is made obvious in my words.

"No parent is perfect, Lucifer," she says, adjusting the skirt of her habit with her thin mahogany fingers. "Not even celestial ones. We sometimes refuse to see what is right in front of us. Because we choose to believe our children are not the monsters they sometimes turn out to be."

"You saw my monster pretty clearly, I would say," I say, hanging my head in shame.

Her warm hand cups my cheek lovingly, like a mother reassuring her child she still loves him after he was caught doing something they weren't meant to. Looking into her eyes, I do not see the disgust or disappointment I always thought I would when I saw my maker again.

"You were never a monster, Lucifer," she smiles up at me. "I told you. Doing bad and being bad are two very different things."

"But I rebelled against you."

"Because you thought it was best for your brothers and sisters. Not because you wanted to, but because you felt it was what you had to do." She sighs heavily again, a deep melancholy filling her eyes. "This is not the case with your brother, though. His reasons are selfish. He thinks he is saving you, but fails to see that you have already been saved by the woman you love."

All of the air rushes out of my lungs at the sound of the one word I have not allowed myself to say about Seraphine. "We are not capable of love." I whisper the words to myself more than her, reminding myself that my kind are not meant to fall in romantic love with another creature.

She throws her head back in laughter. "Everyone falls in love, Lucifer." My brows knit together in confusion. "There is no being alive incapable or unworthy of love. Be it angel, demon, god or goddess, none of us are immune to the pull of our hearts leading us in the direction of the one we were meant to spend forever with. You and I are no exceptions to this."

A small ray of hope shines through the clouds of darkness swirling inside me. "She is mortal, though. Eventually, she will grow old. Death will come for her. And I will remain, forced to face immeasurable eons without her beautiful face. Even just the thought of living a single day without her by my side is like-"

"Hell?" she cuts me off, cocking her eyebrow up at me.

"Yes," I nod, panic gripping my throat tightly.

"Lucifer, you and I both know that Hell is not real."

"But death is. And I am powerless to stop it." The small light of hope begins to fade inside me, leaving nothing but the inky blackness of despair in its wake.

"Powerless?" she huffs. "Are you not still the Devil?"

"I am," I answer, not sure yet what her question means.

"Oh, my sweet child," she croons. "As you have so eloquently put it many times before, every soul has its price."

"Are you saying you would make me a deal?"

"What I am asking is this. What price would her soul be worth to you?"

Her question renews the fading hope inside me. "Anything," I answer, making no attempt to hide my desperate excitement at the chance to save Seraphine. "Everything. Name it and it's yours."

"Would you trade your soul for hers?"

I hesitate, not because I am unwilling to make this trade, but because it seems impossible. "My soul?"

"We all have one," she smiles. "That is the price. Along with the millions upon millions of souls you have collected in your long life."

"I would be mortal, same as she is?"

"No, child," she chuckles softly. "Your immortality is not something I wish to take away from you. You are still an angel and my son, after all." Her face turns very serious as she explains the terms of the deal she is offering. "But you will never again be able to make a deal with a human. Their souls, no matter how wicked or how pure, will be mine to do with as I please. Sickness and age will not touch you. No weapon, mortal or otherwise, will be able to end either of your lives. For you and Seraphine to be able to live without fear of death until the end of forever, that is the price. Are you willing to pay it, Lucifer, Light Bringer of the World?"

"Yes." There is no hesitation in my answer. For the woman I love, I will happily sacrifice this and more.

"Then our deal is made."

God turns to overlook the water once again. I can feel reality starting to seep back into my body. Soon, I will be face to face with my brother again. And the woman I love.

"Oh, and one more thing, my son," she says over her shoulder as she begins to fade from my sight. "Do give your brother my regards."

In an instant, I am back in the bedroom, staring at my brother as his sword is inches away from connecting with my shoulder. I reach forward, no longer feeling as if I am watching from outside my own body, and grab the blade, wrapping my fingers tightly around the sharp metal. Crimson colored blood runs down my arms as I use the blade to pull my bewildered brother closer to me.

"How is this possible?" he says in utter disbelief.

In his confusion, his grip on the hilt loosens. I pull the sword from his hand. Raising it above my head, I watch as knowing fear overcomes my brother.

"Our maker sends their regards." With that, I bring the blade down.

The room explodes again in a bright flash of light. Michael doesn't even scream as his life comes to an end in an instant. I shield my eyes until the light begins to fade away. When I can see clearly again, nothing is left of my brother. For a moment, I worry he may have just disappeared to return to wherever it was he came from. I close my eyes, trying to feel his presence, but feel nothing.

Seraphine sobs softly behind me. Michael's sword falls from my hand to the carpet with a soft thud as I rush to my woman's side. I scoop her up in my arms, covering her beautiful face in tender kisses. Her trembling lips find mine. I taste her salty lips as I hold her tightly against my chest.

Seraphine buries her head in the crook of my neck as I carry her over to the bed. I set her down on the edge, examining her closely for any sign of injury that would need attention. By some miracle, she appears to be completely unscathed.

"Samuel," she says softly, her unblinking eyes looking up at me in search of answers. "What just happened?"

"We have time to talk about everything later," I assure her, placing my hand gently on her cheek.

"How much time?"

"Forever."

"Forever?" she asks, leaning into my palm.

I lean down and brush my lips against hers. "Forever."

EPILOGUE

SERAPHINE

Fifty Years Later

"Do we have a deal, Mr. Jones?"

I hesitate at the sound of Samuel's voice on the other side of his office door talking with a potential new client. I smile to myself, pressing my ear to the wood of the door so I can hear more clearly. I have no doubt Samuel has just made him an offer he will not be able to turn down.

"Let's make it happen," the second voice answers.

My smile widens when I hear the clink of whiskey glasses. I rub my thighs together, my head filling with all the things I know he plans on doing to me later in celebration of closing such an important deal. Even after all these years, he still turns me on as much as he did that day I first met him on that abandoned lot.

I raise my hand again and knock softly on the door. I hear the two men laughing, then the door opens. Samuel's eyes roam my body with less than holy intent. I watch as his gaze traces the deep open v of the soft blue wrap dress I am wearing. When his deep brown eyes meet mine again, I see the faint red glow as his lips curl into a sinister crooked grin.

"Come in, woman," he says, stepping aside for me to enter. "Come meet the newest investor in Heaven's Homeplace Shelter."

"Samuel, you never told me your wife was so stunning," the well-dressed gentleman with salt and pepper hair says as he brings my hand to lips, kissing it chastely. I hear a low growl coming from Samuel as he wraps a protective arm around my waist, pulling my back to his front. I feel his erection lengthening in his slacks.

"Down, boy," I whisper to him over my shoulder. "It's a pleasure to meet you Mr. Jones. Samuel and I are excited to work with you. Together, I am certain we can make a big difference in the lives of so many of the people struggling in the city."

"Well, after your husband told me about the plans you proposed for helping people in

recovery transition from rehab while supporting them on their journey, I knew I wanted to be involved. My sister struggled for a long time with addiction. This donation is in honor of her sobriety."

"My wife and I thank you again," Samuel says. "And congratulations to your sister on ten years clean."

My eyes drift to the framed photo on Samuel's desk. After the incident with his brother, Samuel was adamant on marrying me as soon as possible. I told him I felt wearing white didn't seem appropriate considering my past, but he wouldn't take no for an answer. He told me an angel as beautiful as me should wear white on her wedding day. I agreed under the condition that when we would eventually need to have another wedding to keep up the ruse required to maintain the secrecy of our immortality, I would be allowed to wear whatever I wanted. It took a little creative persuasion on my part, but he eventually agreed. The mind blowing blowjob I gave him as we negotiated might have had a hand in the deal, as well.

The photo is a little bittersweet, though. It marked the last time we saw our dear Eve. God's deal with the Devil inspired her to grant Eve the mercy she had longed for. She grew old, helping hundreds of kids and teens at the shelter in California. After a lifetime spent surrounded by the family she finally found in those children, she passed away peacefully in her sleep. While I miss my friend dearly, my heart is full knowing she was able to find the sweet rest in death she had wanted for so many years.

"I hate to leave good company, but my wife is going to have my hide if I don't make it home before too long." We say our goodbyes to Mr. Jones as we walk him to the door.

After Samuel explained the deal he made for us to be able to have each other for all eternity, I wanted to make sure our long lives would be used to help as many people as we could. He emphatically agreed, saying he had more than enough sins to atone for. We opened the Heaven's Homeplace Foundation to help homeless and struggling families around the world. Now, we plan to help those struggling with addiction with the help they need to get and stay clean. With everything we have done over the past half century, we have saved hundreds of families avoid the life I had endured for so long before I met Samuel.

No sooner than the door closes behind Mr. Jones,

Samuel pounces on me like a wild animal. He crushes his lips to mine, claiming my mouth in the way only he can. My body reacts to him, as it always has from the moment I met him. I match his fiery kiss with the same passion, telling him without words how badly I want him right now. The love neither of us thought we would ever be worthy of wraps itself around us both.

Samuel lifts me in his arms, carrying me down the hallway toward the bedroom of the penthouse we currently reside in. "Woman, this dress is absolutely sinful," he growls in my ear, nipping gently at my lobe. I feel the sharpness of his teeth, a prelude of which Samuel I will be sharing a bed with tonight.

"You would know all about sin, wouldn't you," I giggle in girlish delight.

"You're goddamn right I do," he smirks.

I feel the feathers of his wings ruffle under the fabric of his shirt. A shiver of excitement runs down my spine. I love when he takes me in his human form, but it is nothing in comparison to the absolute feral way he fucks me when he lets the Devil loose.

"Do you have any idea how long I plan on loving you?" he whispers, his voice heavy with sex, as he lays me delicately across our bed.

"Forever?" I ask, untying the front of my dress as he crawls up my body.

"Forever."

Acknowledgments

There are so many people who I would like to thank for helping me bring Samuel and Seraphine to life. Words cannot express how much everyone involved means to me.

To my family, thank you for putting up with the long nights, the half-assed dinners, and the hours spent on my laptop while we watched movies.

Thank you to the Behind The Pages community for keeping me sane and pushing me to continuously better myself.

Thank you to Havoc for allowing me to turn her into the badass female character I always knew she was.

Last but not least, thank you from the bottom of my heart to the man who inspired this entire book. Dante, without you, Samuel would still be just a random line scribbled in a notebook. Your presence in my life has meant more to me in the last three years than anything. You are an amazing human, and I hope you understand how much your friendship means to me. Thank you.

ABOUT THE AUTHOR

Nickole Bryan is a single mom from Mississippi who has been writing most of her life. "I honestly cannot remember a time when I was NOT writing. I use to keep my mother awake at night by staying up late typing on the typewriter she bought me because we couldn't afford a computer at the time." While most of her work in the past has been for screen, her debut novel, Happy Endings, has already received outstanding reviews.

When she isn't writing, Nickole spends her time raising her two kids, Annika and William.

ALSO BY NICKOLE BRYAN

Fallen Series

Falling: Book One

Breaking: Book Two

JustFans Series

Hayden

Happy Endings Duet

Happy Endings: Book One

Happy Endings: Book Two

Standalones

Something Wicked